Early Praise for *Designing Elixir Systems with OTP*

This book has a pragmatic approach that (correctly) prioritizes what *you* need to do over what the frameworks do.

➤ **Dave Thomas**
Author of *Programming Elixir 1.6*

James and Bruce have a way of teaching that distills ideas into easily understandable chunks. *Designing Elixir Systems with OTP* brings their reliable teaching techniques to print. You will walk away with a solid foundation of functional programming design principles and a wheelhouse of simple techniques to help you along your journey.

➤ **Amos King**
CEO, Binary Noggin

This isn't a textbook or a reference. It's a mentorship. It doesn't teach you how to do something. It teaches you how to think about all the things you do in Elixir.

➤ **Adrian P. Dunston**
Senior Software Engineer, Papa, Inc.

This is the book I wish I'd had after getting comfortable with Elixir syntax but was struggling to learn crucial core OTP concepts that make it so powerful. The book uses a great coding example to see each of these concepts in use and would have been invaluable to me while fumbling through learning them on my own. 10/10, would recommend.

➤ **Jon Carstens**
Embedded Systems Engineer, SmartRent

Designing Elixir Systems with OTP

Write Highly Scalable, Self-Healing Software with Layers

James Edward Gray, II
Bruce A. Tate

The Pragmatic Bookshelf

Raleigh, North Carolina

Many of the designations used by manufacturers and sellers to distinguish their products are claimed as trademarks. Where those designations appear in this book, and The Pragmatic Programmers, LLC was aware of a trademark claim, the designations have been printed in initial capital letters or in all capitals. The Pragmatic Starter Kit, The Pragmatic Programmer, Pragmatic Programming, Pragmatic Bookshelf, PragProg and the linking *g* device are trademarks of The Pragmatic Programmers, LLC.

Every precaution was taken in the preparation of this book. However, the publisher assumes no responsibility for errors or omissions, or for damages that may result from the use of information (including program listings) contained herein.

Our Pragmatic books, screencasts, and audio books can help you and your team create better software and have more fun. Visit us at *https://pragprog.com*.

The team that produced this book includes:

Publisher: Andy Hunt
VP of Operations: Janet Furlow
Executive Editor: Dave Rankin
Development Editor: Jacquelyn Carter
Copy Editor: Jasmine Kwytin
Indexing: Potomac Indexing, LLC
Layout: Gilson Graphics

For sales, volume licensing, and support, please contact *support@pragprog.com*.

For international rights, please contact *rights@pragprog.com*.

ISBN-13: 978-1-68050-661-7
Book version: P1.0—December 2019

Contents

Part I — Do Fun Things...

Part II — ...with Big, Loud Worker-Bees

Acknowledgments

This book was a joint effort. It's written in our shared voice. We will begin our thanks in that same voice, then finish with some personal additions.

You are probably pretty familiar with this drill, but it takes a lot more than authors to make a book. We both need to thank our editor Jackie Carter. She is a champion herder of these two cats. We also need to thank our reviewers: Chris Keathly, Amos King, Bruce Williams, Doyle Turner, Adrian P. Dunston, Pedro Medeiros, Jonathan Carstens, Eoghan O'Donnell, Ryan Huber, and Kim Shrier. More so than many other books, we asked them to work through big ideas and no small amount of code while it was still very much under construction. They pushed us back on track whenever we were slipping off.

We want to send special thanks to those pushers of Pimento Cheese, Amos, Anna, and Chris. They were among our first and most ardent supporters, using both the microphone and the electronic pen to advance our book.

Joe Armstrong, a co-creator of the Erlang programming language, died while we were writing this book. Joe had a significant impact on the trajectories of our careers. Joe had a hand in the design of the platform that we now poke around inside of to learn better ways to build software. We're pretty sure Joe would have liked that practice too. We can tell from his conference talks and forum posts that he loved to tinker, explore, and try out new ideas.

Eventually, José Valim came along and expanded Joe's platform in such way that he convinced these old programmers to give it a chance. He's cultivating a core team and a language that combine new ideas with Erlang's inner wisdom. Now there are all new ways to play.

We hope the joy of their creations shine through in these pages.

There's another voice that's quieter than it used to be, but was still critical for this team. Dave Thomas helped us kick around more than a few ideas, and we borrowed some of his as well. We greatly appreciate what you've done for Elixir, and how you shaped these ideas.

James Gray

Joe and José did the hard parts of what you will see ahead and I owe them a lot for sharing their work. Speaking of hard parts, this book was hard for me. I've been writing it for years. It was challenging to find the right way to present these ideas. In fact, I didn't do that! Bruce did. He brought the narrative and cohesion and so much more. He tirelessly reigned in my asides. I am beyond grateful for his guidance and readers should be too.

The rest of my support structure consists of two amazing women: my wife, Dana, and our daughter, Summer. No one will ever really understand why a husband or father asks if he can hide out for years to scribble down some code and prose in the hope that total strangers will read it, but these two bore it with exceptional grace. For me, they made the impossible, possible.

Bruce Tate

Writing this book was hard because of the various people on different sides of ideas that seem important. However, the fun of writing it luckily far outweighed these difficulties. I got to spend time talking about this enjoyable topic with my amazing coauthor and put out something that we both believe in. The partnership was striking in its effectiveness. James has so many deep insights and ideas from poking under every toadstool and flipping over musty stones that others have the sense to leave alone! When we started this effort, I didn't think we'd have enough to say. It turns out that we had just enough!

As always, I want to thank Maggie, my joy and inspiration. You inspire me. Thanks also to Kayla and Julia. I am in awe of the young ladies you've become.

Readers, we'll be on the road and we're bound to run into each other. Don't be shy. Come talk to us and tell us what you think. You make writing fun!

Introduction

In October 2018, we were gathered with some family and friends in a mock Chattanooga train station working to solve a fictional puzzle so we could escape. We had burned through most of our clock and were calling for our next clue. We scrambled to take this last bit of information and translate it to the various combination locks and levers that would let us out of the room. Eventually the host called through the intercom that we'd failed. We'd run out of time.

Roughly two years before, we started working on an advanced book about OTP. We knew that Elixir developers were starting to push the set of tools beyond the basic libraries and books that were on the market at that time. They wanted a way to express increasingly complex code in ways that would scale and hold up to years of revision.

We set ourselves to this effort with a will and fell short. It seemed that we would run out of time, or patience, or will. Some days we came up with outlines that looked like a watered down table of contents for better books. Others we wrote chapters that had nuggets of wisdom presented awkwardly. Sometimes life just got in the way. The train was all but dead and we hauled it back to the station.

Luckily, not every project has a time limit. The last few months seem like we've just been given a clue, the cheat codes that helped us start to pressurize the boiler in this train to get the wheels turning again. These insights helped us break through:

- We didn't want to write strictly about OTP. Sometimes OTP is the *wrong* thing to do. The first half of this book does not cover OTP at all!

- We didn't want to write about simplicity. We wanted to write about revealing complexity piece by piece in layers.

- We wanted to present material that developers could remember and take with them.

With these ideas in mind, we rebooted the project. The boiler pressure built enough that our wheels started to turn and we pulled out of the station once again.

Worker-Bee-Driven Design

James came up with a great way to generalize the layers for a typical OTP project, which led to the sentence "Do fun things with big, loud worker-bees" to remember the layers: data, functions, tests, boundaries, lifecycles, workers. We shared these ideas with some trusted advisors and they resonated strongly. We began to experience an unfamiliar feeling of blessed momentum!

All at once, with that system of layering we had the overarching structure for our table of contents. We could finally imagine the book that Elixir developers have long desired. The system of layers gave us a framework for expressing the deep wisdom we've collected and the simple layers let us express those ideas in a way our readers could understand and digest piecemeal.

James picked the perfect project for the book and we could immediately imagine what the layers in our software would look like and how to present each piece to the user. As we used all of these layers together in the context of a complex project, it *felt right*. We had discovered WDD, or worker-bee-driven design. As we continue to write software, we can testify that the approaches work.

We hope these layers have the same impact on your software that it has had on our book. We hope they feel like cheat codes that completely unlock your thought processes so you can escape some of the concurrency ceremony and move on to the hard pieces of your problem.

Who Should Read This Book

Hopefully, you have a rough idea of the work we'll be doing together. We'll examine design through layers.

In this book, we're addressing intermediate and advanced programmers who want a better understanding of how to design Elixir projects. We'll offer advice in this book that may conflict with concepts you've seen elsewhere, but that's OK. You can take what you like and leave the rest behind.

If you are an Elixir beginner, this book will be for you eventually, but not yet. You should take advantage of one of the many excellent Elixir books and courses available, including *Programming Elixir 1.6 [Tho18]* by Dave Thomas.

If you would like to focus on programming user interfaces and want to skip the heavy back-end designs, you'd be better off reading *Programming Phoenix 1.4 [TV19]*. Similarly, if you're concerned with pure database programming, *Programming Ecto [WM19]* is the book you'll want to check out instead.

Online Resources

You can get the code from the book page on the Pragmatic Bookshelf website.[1] We hope that when you find errors or suggestions that you will report them via the book's errata page.[2]

If you like the book we hope you'll take the time to let others know about it. Reviews matter, and one tweet or post from you is worth ten of ours! We're both on Twitter, and tweet regularly. Find James at @jeg2 and Bruce at @redrapids. You can also drop notes to @pragprog!

We're excited to head down the tracks with you. We hope you enjoy it as much as we have.

James E. Gray, II and Bruce A. Tate
December 2019

---

1. https://pragprog.com/book/jgotp
2. https://pragprog.com/titles/jgotp/errata

CHAPTER 1

Build Your Project in Layers

Don't let anyone tell you differently. Building great software is hard, and Elixir's not a silver bullet. Though it makes dealing with processes *easier*, concurrent code will never be *easy*. If your checklist includes intimidating scalability requirements, performance consistency under load, or highly interactive experiences or the like, programming gets harder still. In this book, we won't shy away from these demands.

If you're like us, you found a valuable companion in Elixir, with some characteristics you believe can help you with some of these challenges, even if you don't fully understand it. Perhaps Elixir is your first functional language, as it is for many of us. You may need some guidance for how to choose your data structures or organize your functions. Or, you might have found several ways to deal with concurrency and need some advice on which approach to use.

We can tell you definitively that you're not alone and we're here to help. We won't offer panaceas, or full solutions to toy problems that have general advice about *design*. We will offer some mental models for how to deal with complexity piece by piece.

With most any new endeavor, progress comes at a price. Our first payment is a willingness to change.

We Must Reimagine Design Choices

We believe good software design is about building layers, so perhaps the most important aspect of this book is *helping good programmers understand where layers should go and how they work*. Some of the techniques that we used when the internet was young are not the ones we'll be using into the future, but take heart. This author team doesn't have all of the answers, but both of us have a strong corpus to draw from.

Some of our inspiration comes from the past. Throughout this book, we're going to distill much of the conventional wisdom from functional programmers and we're not shy about crossing language boundaries to learn. We're going to draw on the expertise of Elixir programmers, including many of the people who shaped the language as it was formed.

We'll also draw inspiration from Erlang, Clojure, and Elm for algorithms and techniques to solve problems similar to the ones we're facing as we determine what the right set of layers should be. We'll rely heavily on Erlang, especially the OTP framework that helps manage concurrency state and lifecycle.

This book is about design, and because Elixir heavily uses OTP, we must address how to construct layers around an OTP program. Let's define that term quickly with a brief generality. OTP is a library that uses processes and layers to make it easy to build concurrent, self-healing software. Throughout the book, we'll deepen that understanding.

In this brief journey together, we will show you how to write effective Elixir by showing you how to use layers to hide complex features until you need to think about them. We'll extend our layers to take advantage of OTP, offering some intuition for how it works and some guidance for how to incorporate it into your layered designs.

If you find some tools to improve that skill, even if you don't use every technique in this book, you'll be much better positioned to create good Elixir code that takes full advantage of the wide variety of libraries and frameworks in the Elixir ecosystem.

The first question you may be asking is which layers you should build. In the sections that follow, we'll offer some guidance to help you choose.

Choose Your Layers

The layers we will present to write a typical project are not set in stone. Instead, they are a rough scaffold, a framework for thinking about solutions to common design problems. We're not slaves to these systems but they help to free us from dealing with mechanical details so that we can focus on solving problems.

We recommend the software layers: data structures, a functional core, tests, boundaries, lifecycle, and workers. Not every project will have all of these layers, but some will. It's your job as the author of a codebase to decide which layers are worth the price and which ones to eliminate. It's a lot to remember, so use this sentence as a mnemonic:

Do fun things with big, loud worker-bees.

The first letter of the essential words in the sentence match the first letters in our layers: data, functional core, tests, boundaries, lifecycles, workers. You can see how they all fit together in the following figure:

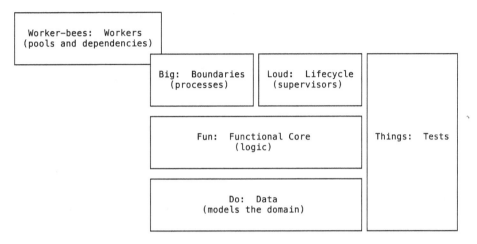

Do fun things with big, loud worker-bees.

In this chapter, we will explore each layer in detail. We'll call each unit of software you build that honors these concepts a *component*.

To help you understand what each of these layers do, we're going to build two components in this book. The first will be a trivial counter. We know you understand how counters work, but building this component will help you internalize the *design framework* we've established, and what each of the layers means.

The next component, a project called Mastery, will be much more complex, and will comprise the whole rest of the book. It will be a quiz, but not a typical one. This quiz will tailor itself as the user answers questions. Its purpose will be to help you learn to *use that design framework in context* to build a project with real complexity.

Let's get started with that first component, the counter. Rather, let's *not* get started. It always pays to think first.

Think Before You Start

This isn't as much a layer in our framework as a philosophy for coding. Most programmers don't think enough before opening the editor. It's healthy to start every problem with whatever tools help you think. It may just mean propping your feet up on a desk; it may be spending a little bit of time with a whiteboard or even a pen and paper. Testing zealots like us believe bugs are less expensive to fix before they reach the customer. We'll take this idea further. Bugs are cheapest to catch before you write your first line of code.

At this stage, your first goal is to understand how to break down the major components in your system. Within the Elixir community, you won't find any single answer to how fine you should break down your components.

Here's the thing. If you think of OTP as a way to encapsulate data, or even objects, you're going to get it wrong. Elixir processes work best when they span a few modules that belong together. Breaking your processes up too finely invites integrity problems the same way that global variables do.

We believe that whenever possible, concepts that belong together should be packaged together as part of the same component. For example, we'd rather wrap a process around a *chess game* as a standalone component than have each *piece* in its own process, so we can enforce the integrity of the board at the *game level*.

Our counter is a standalone component that we'll use to count things in isolation. The data is an integer, does not need to persist through a failure or restart. The counter has a two function API to increment the counter and get the value. We only have a single component so we don't have to *divide responsibilities*.

We'll make the critical assumption that persisting state is unimportant and we don't have to worry about guaranteed delivery of messages, even across restarts, but our counter should track a value transiently, and that value should be available to other processes. Such state is *ephemeral*. Freedom from persistence allows us much more flexibility than we'd otherwise experience. Elixir is extremely good at managing ephemeral state such as counters and caches. In later chapters, you'll see a good way to add persistence to a component as we deal with the second component.

Create a Mix Project

With those details firmly in place, we can create our software. You might have noticed that until now, we've steadfastly avoided the word "application." There's a reason for that decision. The term is overloaded. To any given Elixir developer, an application might be the thing you:

- Build with OTP
- Create when you type mix new
- Create when you type mix phx.new
- Deploy

And each of these, in some context, is right. We're going to refrain from using "application" in the context of the thing we're creating with mix new. That thing is a *project*. Let's create one now.

Create a new project from your OS console. Type mix new counter and change into the counter directory. We are finally ready to build our first layer.

Begin with the Right Datatypes

The "data" layer has the simple data structures your functions will use. Just as an artist needs to learn to use the colors on their palette, Elixir developers need to learn the best ways to mix the data structures. Every programmer making a transition to functional programming needs to understand its impact on data design.

In this book, we won't tell you what maps or lists are, but we will provide an overview of what kinds of datatypes to choose for selected tasks and how you can weave them together into a good functional data strategy. We'll give you some dos and don'ts for the most common datatypes, and provide you some tips for choosing good ways to express the concepts in your program as data.

Our counter's datatype couldn't be simpler. It's an integer. Normally, you'll spend much more time thinking about your data than we do here. You'll likely begin to code up the major entities in your system. We don't need to do that for our counter because Elixir already has the integer, and it already supports the kinds of things we'll do to it.

As this book grows, we'll spend a good amount of time working through data structures. Our focus will be primarily in three areas:

- We'll look at what's idiomatic and efficient in Elixir.
- We'll review how our structures will influence the designs of our functions.
- We'll consider some of the trade-offs around cohesion, meaning how closely we group related bits of data.

When the data structure is right, the functions holding the algorithms that do things can seem to write themselves. Get them wrong and it doesn't really matter how good a programmer you are; your functions will feel clumsy and awkward.

Since we don't have any custom data structures, we can move on. Let's write some functions.

Build Your Functional Core

Now we'll finally start coding. Our functional core is what some programmers call the business logic. This inner layer does not care about any of the machinery related to processes; it does not try to preserve state; and it has no side effects (or, at least, the bare minimum that we must deal with). It is made up of functions.

Our goal is to deal with complexity in isolation. Make no mistake, processes and side effects add complexity. Building our core allows us to isolate the inherent complexity of our *domain* from the complexity of the *machinery* we need to manage processes, handle side effects, and the like.

In a chess game, this logic would have functions that take a board, move an individual piece, and return an updated board. It may also have a function to take a board with all of its pieces and calculate the relative strength of a position. In a calculator, the core would handle all of the numeric operators for the calculator.

Let's look at a specific example, our counter. Our business logic will count numbers. This code should be as side effect free as we can make it. It should observe two rules:

- It must not have side effects, meaning it should not alter the state of its environment in any way.

- A function invoked with the same inputs will always return the same outputs.

Our counter's business logic increments a value. Let's write that inner functional core now. Crack open lib/counter/core.ex and make it look like this:

```
GettingStarted/counter/lib/counter/core.ex
defmodule Counter.Core do
  def inc(value) do
    value + 1
  end
end
```

Though you can't yet behold the power of the fully operational counter, the business logic makes it easy to track exactly what is happening. Our public API has two functions: one to advance the counter and one to return state. The process we'll use to manage state doesn't belong here so we need only the inc function. Let's take it for a quick spin. Open it with iex -S mix, like this:

```
iex(1)> Counter.Core.inc(1)
```

Documentation and Typespecs

Before we dive into code, let's say a brief word about documentation. We'll mainly strip out the module docs and doc tests when we initially work on a project because we want to keep a tight feedback loop. A book is a poor place for comments and documentation fixtures in code because prose serves that role. In practice, when code reaches a fairly mature point, we'll add typespecs and module docs, and possibly even doc tests if they make sense. We also made the tough decision to remove type-specs because books are about trade-offs between space and concept. We believe the story arc flows better without them.

All of this is to say documentation and typespecs are important, but do what works for you. If you want to read more, check out *Adopting Elixir [Tat18]*.

That's all our functional core needs, just the functions that manipulate our data structure. If you want to see this code in the context of a program, spin up the following program:

```elixir
defmodule Clock do
  def start(f) do
    run(f, 0)
  end

  def run(your_hearts_desire, count) do
    your_hearts_desire.(count)
    new_count = Counter.Core.inc(count)
    :timer.sleep(1000)
    run(your_hearts_desire, new_count)
  end
end
```

If you want to run this much, open up a new IEx shell because we'll have to kill the following one after running the timer since it loops forever. Then pick what you want to do every cycle by passing whichever function your heart desires into run, like this:

```elixir
iex> Clock.start(fn(tick) -> IO.puts "The clock is ticking with #{tick}" end)
The clock is ticking with 1
The clock is ticking with 2
The clock is ticking with 3
...
```

And you'll have to kill that session with hot fire because it loops forever. Still, you can see the way we build our inner layer into a functional core.

We've addressed the data and functional core in "Do fun things"; we will come back to tests. For now, we understand that our counter must be more than a simple library. Counters exist to count and that means saving state. It's time to address the process machinery, the "big, loud worker-bees" part of our mnemonic. We'll start with a boundary layer.

Establish Your Boundaries

The boundary layer deals with side effects and state. This layer is where you'll deal with processes, and where you'll present your API to the outside world. In Elixir, that means OTP.

We want to dispel the notion that each time you type mix new, you must reach for a GenServer, the fundamental abstraction in OTP. The first way to win the boundary game is not to play. Some projects don't need boundary layers at all. If you're building a library of functions that doesn't need processes, don't add them. Your code is a library and can present an API that serves your purposes just fine. There's no boundary; no GenServer; no lifecycle. Your library will serve other software systems that provide this infrastructure, but it need not introduce those concepts.

With that disclaimer out of the way, if you're dealing with state in Elixir, you'll often use processes in conjunction with recursion and message passing, and you'll usually use OTP GenServers to provide that concept.

It's time to be a little more precise with our definition of boundary. A *boundary layer* is:

- The machinery of processes, message passing, and recursion that form the heart of concurrency in Elixir systems
- An API of plain functions that hides that machinery from clients

We typically call the collective machinery a *server*, the code that calls that server an *API*, and the code that calls that API a *client*. In OTP's case, the server in that boundary layer is called a *GenServer*, which is an abbreviation for Generic Server.

In this section, rather than using OTP, we'll build similar concepts from scratch. We do this to demystify OTP and show you exactly what's happening under the hood, so when it's time to build your boundary layer with OTP, you'll understand exactly what's happening.

Now we'll code a process that looks a little like the clock in the previous example. Our new counter will have two functions: one to tick the counter and another to get the current count. It's surprisingly easy. Crack open /lib/counter/server.ex and key this in:

GettingStarted/counter/lib/counter/server.ex
```
defmodule Counter.Server do
  def run(count) do
    new_count = listen(count)
    run(new_count)
  end
```

We define a module called server. Our server is just a process that exposes a service layer. Don't get hung up in today's baggage about the name. We're calling it a server to mirror Elixir's terminology, and it means *a process that provides a service*. We save state by running a loop, with each iteration of the loop containing the new state. In the midst of our loop, we invite users to send a message to our server, a message which may change the state.

Now, to code the listen function, the heart of our loop:

GettingStarted/counter/lib/counter/server.ex
```
  def listen(count) do
    receive do
      {:tick, _pid} ->
        Counter.Core.inc(count)
      {:state, pid} ->
        send(pid, {:count, count})
        count
    end
  end
end
```

Here's the magic. The receive block allows us to interact with the server at each iteration of the loop. The tick message uses the functional core to calculate the new state. The listen function sends the state message back to the server and returns the count. All that remains is to wrap all of these features up into a friendly API, which we'll put in lib/counter.ex, like this:

GettingStarted/counter/lib/counter.ex
```
defmodule Counter do
  def start(initial_count) do
    spawn( fn() -> Counter.Server.run(initial_count) end )
  end

  def tick(pid) do
    send pid, {:tick, self()}
  end
```

```
def state(pid) do
  send pid, {:state, self()}
  receive do

    {:count, value} -> value
  end
end
end
```

Our API interacts with our process with spawn, send, and receive, just as you'd expect. We track each counter process with a pid, which we keep as we spawn a new process. The tick and state functions are ridiculously simple. They send messages to the server, and retrieve a response if we expect one back.

And that's it. We can interact with our counter. Either recompile or restart IEx with iex -S mix, and you're ready to play:

```
iex(1)> counter_pid = Counter.start(0)
#PID<0.112.0>
iex(2)> Counter.tick(counter_pid)
{:tick, #PID<0.112.0>}
iex(3)> Counter.state(counter_pid)
1
iex(4)> Counter.tick(counter_pid)
{:tick, #PID<0.112.0>}
iex(5)> Counter.tick(counter_pid)
{:tick, #PID<0.112.0>}
iex(6)> Counter.state(counter_pid)
3
```

The counter_pid points to a process, and that process is our homemade GenServer. We can interact with it directly by sending it messages with our API layer. Together those two concepts make up our boundary layer. Notice that the sends and receives are hidden from us. At this level of abstraction, we just know that we have an API endpoint that counts.

OTP and State

We built some boilerplate to use recursion and message passing to manage state. The OTP GenServer does precisely that. It creates a process and loops over some state. Then other processes can modify that state by sending the GenServer messages.

In Elixir, OTP uses the magic of macros and functions to make all of this available with little ceremony: the recursive loop, the message passing, and more. They hide many of the messy details from you. It gives the user control of the receive_message function by calling functions called callbacks in your code. We'll get into the details, but for now, understand that OTP is an Elixir feature that uses concurrency, recursion, and process primitives to track processes and manage state. It also has features we'll need but have not yet discussed to handle circumstances like graceful startup and shutdown.

Few creatures are as mysterious or misunderstood as the OTP server. Consider the name. Ask a grizzled Elixir or Erlang veteran what OTP means and you'll get a story that goes something like this:

> Long ago, the acronym stood for "open telephone platform", but it doesn't have anything to do with telephony. So now, it doesn't stand for anything.

Or check out the anchor concept, the GenServer. Forget that *gen* is abbreviated. The *server* word is confusing enough as it is because these GenServers are abstractions that usually don't have anything to do with network communication at all.

It's no wonder that this concept is poorly understood by the bulk of programmers that enter the Elixir ecosystem, even though the concepts underneath the architecture are stunningly simple. Remember the loop and the counter. That's the heart of OTP.

Since variables in functional languages are *immutable*, we can't just change them when we want to change state. Instead, OTP uses function *arguments* to represent our state, and have a recursive loop just calling itself with a new state as shown in the following diagram. All our counter needs to do is specify a *call* message to our process, which increments the counter and specifies the new value for the state.

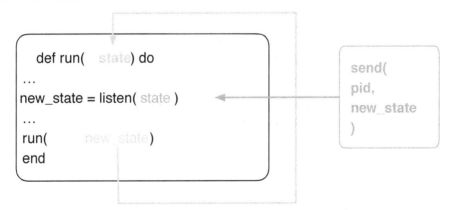

```
def run(    state) do
...
new_state = listen( state )
...
run(    new_state)
end
```

```
send(
pid,
new_state
)
```

Keep Your Functional Core Separate

A surprising number of Elixir developers get tripped up at this point. It's tempting to wrap up the details of your business logic in the state management. Doing so conflates two concerns: *organization* and *concurrency*. We'll use *modules* not *processes* to organize our code so basic strategy changes won't necessarily lead to changing your core business logic. We'll use an API that hides messaging. If we need to, we can then wrap that core in a process layer to provide concurrent performance and error isolation.

If we wanted to, we could also add some code to do tests, manage the counter's lifecycle, and perhaps pool resources. These bits of function and configuration would be part of a boundary, but our counter does not really need them. All of these layers are working together to form a single working unit, and that's the API we'll expose to the rest of the world.

As we dive in to more sophisticated examples, we'll tap the depths of functional composition as well. We'll show you the nuances of coding and testing these kinds of solutions, designing your functions to be friendly to Elixir's main units of composition, pipelines and with/1. For now, we have a promising start so it's time to move on.

Test Your Code

One of the benefits of structuring your project into core and boundary layers is that our coding organization will simplify testing. With a basic API layer that does most of the business logic, you'll be able to write tests to thoroughly exercise your business code should you choose to do so. You'll be able to represent your testing concepts in any way you choose, and we'll discuss a few strategies as the book evolves.

We will focus on unit testing here with ExUnit, but the same principles apply to property-based testing, a philosophy that allows you to specify properties about your code so that the computer can generate many different tests. For now, let's write a simple test for our counter. We'll start with the business logic.

Since we have only a single function, testing it should go quickly. Open up test/counter_test.exs and make it look like this:

```
GettingStarted/counter/test/counter_test.exs
defmodule CounterTest do
  use ExUnit.Case
  test "inc increments an integer value" do
    assert Counter.Core.inc(1) == 2
  end
end
```

We dropped the doctest that appears by default for now, but we could add it again later after our code stabilizes, should we choose to do so. We won't talk too much about testing philosophies yet. We'll just mention that testing core code is easier and more predictable, so it often receives the bulk of the test focus.

Testing the boundary layer is important, but it's also pretty simple because we'll use the outer API to do so. That test looks like this:

```
GettingStarted/counter/test/counter_api_test.exs
defmodule CounterApiTest do
  use ExUnit.Case

  test "use counter through API" do
    pid = Counter.start(0)
    assert Counter.state(pid) == 0

    Counter.tick(pid)
    Counter.tick(pid)

    count = Counter.state(pid)
    assert count == 2
  end
end
```

Notice that we're testing by interacting with our servers via an API, the way our client users would. Sometimes, testing using only this API layer is the right thing to do.

We're just getting started and you can already tell that testing the functional core will be easy because we don't have to deal with external conditions. Since that's where most of the logic should be, it will give you a good opportunity to do as much work as possible before you start integrating components.

That's a pretty good start on the testing layer, but you can learn more, starting with the ExUnit documentation.[1] Testing your components will often mean using techniques to isolate elements of your code, and clean out messages in your queue.

Now that we've dealt with data, functions, tests, and boundaries, it's time to focus on lifecycle.

Plan Your Lifecycle

We're going to break with tradition and use the word *lifecycle* instead of *supervisor*. Most Elixir developers think of Elixir's supervision as a way to handle failure, and it's easy to see why. Some Erlang deployments using OTP have been up for years at a time. If you've been telling yourself that "supervisors are about failure," we want to help you reshape that idea.

---

1. https://hexdocs.pm/ex_unit/ExUnit.html

To illustrate, let's look at some holes in our Counter component. Look at the start function in our counter again:

GettingStarted/counter/lib/counter.ex
```elixir
defmodule Counter do
  def start(initial_count) do
    spawn( fn() -> Counter.Server.run(initial_count) end )
  end

  def tick(pid) do
    send pid, {:tick, self()}
  end
  def state(pid) do
    send pid, {:state, self()}
    receive do

      {:count, value} -> value
    end
  end
end
```

This code has a problem. If the code crashes at any time, the counter will not recover and components using it will likely fail too. If we were to continue to build out our own personal OTP, we would have to start a linked process. Then we'd wait for a DOWN or EXIT message and restart the process with a clean, good state.

Supervisors are about starting and stopping cleanly, whether you have a single server or a bunch of them. Once you can start cleanly and detect failure, you can get failover almost for free. When a customer support person says "Did you try turning it off and on again?", they are using lifecycle to recover from failure, whether you're working with a TV or a desktop computer program. They are making a good bet that shutting things down cleanly and starting with a known good state is a powerful way to heal broken things.

Here, then, is the premise of the whole supervision strategy underneath Elixir. Get the lifecycle right and you have a very good chance to get failure recovery right as well.

We'll look at our lifecycle in exactly these terms in Chapter 7, Customize Your Lifecycle, on page 131. We'll rely on OTP to do the heavy lifting. We'll define how to start things and stop them correctly. Whether you're bringing your system up after a deploy or after a failure doesn't really matter.

Elixir will give us the tools to handle complexity, including a strategy and ordering for starting your code, shutting things down correctly, and, yes, handling failure. Our simple counter has a simple lifecycle, a broken one. Failure will result in the failure of our counter, and possibly failure of the systems that rely on it. When we build our next component, one based on OTP, we'll fix those limitations.

Here's the point to the lifecycle layer. One of the core ideas in Elixir that passed straight down from Erlang is that lifecycle is a fundamental principle of design.

It's time to move on to the next layer.

Invoke Your Workers

The workers are the different processes in your component. Generally, you'll start with a flat design having a single worker and decide where you need to be more sophisticated. As your design evolves you will possibly see places that you need to add workers, for cleaning up lifecycles or for concurrently dividing work. Connection pools are workers; tasks and agents can be as well.

Believe it or not, our Counter component is not the simplest possible. We could have a library with a counter API but no state at all. That program would not have any workers. Our counter has a single worker, one we use to encapsulate state with OTP. Still, we don't have to yet consider how to efficiently partition work, but Elixir will give us some of the best tools in the world for dealing with these kinds of issues.

When it's time, we'll have several options to summon workers, from unsupervised processes and simple tasks on the simple end of the spectrum to processes spawned from dynamic supervisors on the other. We also have to consider how to partition workers. Sometimes we'll want to start a process per user such as web requests, and other times we'll have a consistent pool of processes to serve requests such as a database connection pool.

As you can imagine, this section is closely related to the last one. Once you introduce a process, you must also consider its lifecycle. We considered grouping them together, but we view supervision as primarily a *lifecycle discussion* and process control as a *process organization discussion*.

There you have it. Our counter is done and you've seen all of our layers. Let's wrap up, and then we'll be ready to go into more detail about each layer in turn.

Do Fun Things with Big, Loud Worker-Bees

We've addressed all of the major concepts in our mental framework. You can remember them all with the sentence above. The sentence is a mental mnemonic for data, functions, tests, boundaries, lifecycle, and workers.

Look. We know not every program needs every one of these layers. For example, if you just need a couple of temperature functions and you try to create all of these layers, your project is going to stink. Not all components need all of these layers, but if you teach yourself to think in these terms, you'll understand exactly how to think about Elixir's development.

Elixir is probably different from languages you have used before. It is functional, with great language features to support concurrency, and great abstractions for dealing with both lifecycle and state. All of that power across so many dimensions comes with risk of building so much complexity that you can't manage it all. In this chapter, we introduced principles for thinking about development to allow you to introduce features and abstractions in layers, so you do not have to think about too much at any given time.

Data, Functions, Tests

Remember these with the mnemonic "do fun things."

Our first three steps relate to the internal building blocks of your project. They are datatypes, functions, and tests. We construct the datatypes that will later guide the structure of our component and the interactions between our functions. We divide our functions along the obvious lines of purpose, but we don't stop there. We also separate our core from our boundary layers. Finally, we use tests to verify what we've done. Our test layers use conventional techniques to test our core, boundary, supervision, and workers.

Boundaries, Lifecycles, Workers

Remember these by thinking of "big, loud worker-bees."

Our next three steps relate to how the components of your system work together. We begin with the important boundaries within your solution. We built this layer into our counter from scratch to show you how OTP works underneath. Getting these interfaces right is the secret to dealing with only small pieces of complexity at a time. The boundary API for our counter was clean, with only very small hints to the implementation underneath.

We use the term *lifecycle* rather than *failover* because you must get lifecycles right to build in failover, deployments, startup, and clean shutdown. Our counter built only a broken version of lifecycle but we'll show how to do the same with OTP as the book progresses.

Finally, we talked about dividing our work. Our counter had a single process so we didn't need to do more, though we did point out some of the other features in your tool box. Elixir and its libraries provides tasks, agents, worker pools, and the like.

With the groundwork behind us, in the next chapter we can dive into the first step! Turn the page and we'll dig deeply into datatypes.

Part I

Do Fun Things...

In this part of the book, we'll look at the first half of the sentence, "Do fun things with big, loud worker-bees." Data, functions, and tests are the layers that focus on the parts of your program that don't require supervision, OTP, or any other process machinery at all.

CHAPTER 2

Know Your Elixir Datatypes

Since our book is about design, it's about layers, and all other layers depend on the data layer. The next two chapters will focus on the "D" for "data" in the sentence "Do fun things with big, loud worker-bees." In this chapter, we'll look at Elixir's implementation of the foundational datatypes, and in the next chapter you'll see how to use them as building blocks in the data structures that will form your data layer.

You may be primed to "get to the good stuff," the functions or the OTP. Give us a moment to talk you out of that mindset.

In Elixir, the data *is* the good stuff. If you have worked with functional languages before, you know that they work differently under the hood than what you'd find in other languages. Those who love programming contests or analyzing algorithms know that your data structures drive the shape of your design. If you want to get the most out of this language, you need to know the best Elixir datatype to employ in each situation—which structures are the fastest to copy, and which ones allow the smoothest updates. You need to understand how functional programs will impact your choices and why certain structures most elegantly represent the problems you're likely to encounter.

In that spirit, in this chapter we'll tell you more than simply what a datatype does. We'll describe the trade-offs so that if you're building a structure that needs to be updated often, you can choose between maps, lists, and tuples. It's a short chapter, but a tough one. Come with focus. It's going to be fun.

Not all languages are alike, but languages in different families often have similar characteristics. Functional languages like Elixir tend to support the same kinds of datatypes. Functional lists are almost always linked lists because of the ease of traversing them with functions and the required internal implementation for efficiency. Functional languages generally support fixed-length lists like Elixir's tuples. Elixir also supports maps and structs for dealing with key-value pairs, strings, and charlists for dealing with text, and bitstrings for dealing with bitwise data, as well as some other complex types and primitive ones, as you can see in the following figure:

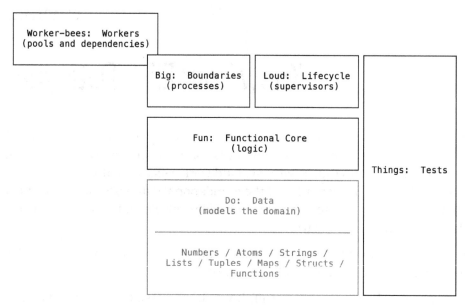

There's a lot of ground to cover, including the datatypes in this figure. Let's start with the most simple building blocks, our primitive types.

Primitive Types

Elixir supports a short list of primitive types, including booleans, floats, integers, atoms, and references. We don't have much guidance for primitive types since for the most part they behave much like they do in other languages. We do have a couple of thoughts, though.

Numbers

Elixir numbers are integers and floats. Remember that floats are estimates.[1] Consider this example:

```
iex(1)> 0.1 + 0.2
0.30000000000000004
```

---

1. https://floating-point-gui.de/

Therefore, unless you're in a position to profit illegally, prefer integers or decimals over floats when you can. Here are a few places that strategy might make, er, sense:

- If you have a choice, store money in cents.
- Use div() and rem() to get integer division rather than /.
- make_ref() is a function that returns a reference,[2] an Elixir type that is typically used as a globally unique identifier. These references are generally better than numbers for identifying things.

With numbers behind us, let's move on to atoms, the next primitive datatype.

Atoms

Since languages such as Java don't support atoms, it's probably worth talking through where to use them versus strings. In general, atoms are for naming concepts. The keys in a struct, the colors your API supports, or the mix environment are examples. Atoms are quite efficient, taking a single word, plus a lookup table.

Atoms are different than strings internally. Two different strings in Elixir with the same contents may or may not be the same, but two different atoms *are* the same object. This concept is the atom's greatest strength and its greatest weakness.

The strength is the representation of concise concepts efficiently. One atom is one integer. That efficiency carries a potential trap, though. If you choose to use atoms for user data or generated concepts, the table that maps atoms onto integers will keep growing until you run out of memory. Exhausting the atom table will crash the BEAM, the virtual machine that runs all Elixir code. Therefore, it's important to use atoms only for things with a finite set of possible values, even a relatively small set of values.

Lists

One of the most important data structures in Elixir is the list. *If you're thinking about skipping this section because lists are arrays, please stop and read on.* In Elixir, lists are singly linked, meaning that each node of a list points to the next node. That's extremely different than arrays. Arrays make random access cheap, but traversing lists takes longer.

Here's the main point. In Elixir, a list with n elements is actually n different lists. Said another way, you can accurately represent [1, 2, 3] with a list construction operator, called *cons cells*, like this:

---

2. https://hexdocs.pm/elixir/Kernel.html#make_ref/0

```
[ 1 |
    [ 2 |
        [ 3 | [] ] ] ]
```

We have four different lists. Each list starts with an open bracket and any code can bind to any one of those individual lists. Each | operator will create a brand-new list, leaving the tail intact. Depending on how you use these lists, this construction actually comes into play as you navigate your various access strategies and modifications. Let's see why.

Order Of

As we discuss the performance of algorithms, let's take a brief moment to describe a key indicator of performance, order-of (sometimes called Big O). It's a brief rough description of the efficiency of an algorithm. If something is O(1) for a list, that means it has one step regardless of the size of the list. (Elixir's hd function is O(1).) If a function is O(n) for a list n elements long, that means the algorithm has n steps. It also means that some algorithms grow very quickly or slowly with the number of elements in a list. The efficiency of algorithms, then, follows the rules of math. From fastest to slowest, we'll see algorithms with O(1), O(log n), and O(n).

Random Access in Lists

Lists are built head-first as you'll see in the figure on page 25. Accessing them by the head is extremely efficient. Pattern matching on the head is O(1). Random access is far less so. To access the third element of a list you need to access the first two. That kind of expense can add up quickly if you're working with recursion and long lists.

Updating Lists

Updating lists has similar characteristics, but also some surprising efficiencies. Adding an element to the head is O(1). Elixir doesn't need to copy anything, it just makes a new head and points it at the existing list you're adding to. This may be surprising to you. For example, changing the third element of a list is more efficient than you might expect, whether you're measuring memory or time. Let's say you want to replace an item in a list:

```
iex> list = [1, 2, 3, 4, 5]
[1, 2, 3, 4, 5]
iex> replaced = List.replace_at(list, 2, 0)
[1, 2, 0, 4, 5]
```

Each list in Elixir is a head pointed to another list, so [1, 2, 3, 4, 5] is actually six different lists. One of those is [4, 5]. The replace_at/3 function must discard the first half of the list, but it's not a *complete* replacement.

The following figure shows what's happening. We can actually leave the sublist -4-5 alone, since it's at the tail and can serve both lists in memory. We need only copy the first two elements of the list.

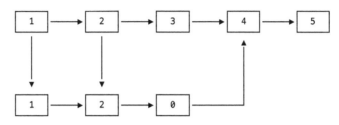

List.replace_at([1, 2, 3, 4, 5], 2, 0)

That means though replacements are more expensive in functional languages than their imperative counterparts, the story is not as bad as it otherwise might be. You do need to be careful, though. When accessing long lists, the head is far better than the tail, and using algorithms that avoid copying altogether are better than algorithms that don't.

Elixir Is Lazy When You Need It to Be

Though we don't talk much about it, streams provide some wonderful properties because Elixir can be lazy when you want it to be. Lazy functional languages do exactly what you think. They delay execution of a sequence until the values are actually needed. The Stream module is the implementation of Elixir's laziness. It's full of functions that don't compute values until they are needed. Elixir's streams let you deal with large blocks of data and infinite sequences, while avoiding unnecessary computation.

When you're dealing with very large datasets, data of indeterminate size, or data from external sources, you'll want to use streams. If you want to delay execution for computed lists, you'll also be using a stream.

We've taken an initial look at lists and streams. Next is one of Elixir's most recent additions, the map.

Maps and Structs

The map has rapidly become the go-to data structure for Elixir programmers. For the purposes of this section, we're going to treat maps and structs as basically the same thing. In IEx, you can see that a struct is actually implemented as a map. Let's take a peek under the hood:

```
iex(1)> defmodule User do
...(1)>    defstruct [:name, :email]
...(1)> end
{:module, User, ...}
iex(2)> map = %User{}
%User{email: nil, name: nil}
iex(3)> is_map(map)
true
iex(4)> map.__struct__
User
```

So a User is actually a map. All structs have a __struct__ field that plain Elixir maps don't have. Let's look at the functions User supports. In IEx, type "User." and then type tab, twice:

```
iex(5)> User.__struct__
__struct__/0    __struct__/1
iex(6)> User.__struct__
%User{email: nil, name: nil}
iex(7)> User.__struct__ name: "James"
%User{email: nil, name: "James"}
```

The defstruct macro adds the __struct__ function to User with two arities. The zero arity function creates a default struct and the second takes a list of key-value pairs.

One capability of structs that's often missed is the @enforce_keys module attribute. You can use it to force the specification of one or more fields when creating a new struct, like this:

```
iex(1)> defmodule User do
...(1)>    @enforce_keys [:name]
...(1)>    defstruct [:name, :age]
...(1)> end
{:module, User,..., %User{age: nil, name: nil}}
iex(2)> %User{age: 25}
** (ArgumentError) the following keys must also be given
    when building struct User: [:name]
    expanding struct: User.__struct__/1
    iex:2: (file)
```

We specify a key to enforce, and then try to create a struct without it. We get an exception. That's a handy trick to make sure default values don't slip by and cause data integrity problems within your codebase. Even with this extra enforcement, when you use a struct you're dealing with a Map. The *characteristics* of maps and structs are the same because the *implementation* is the same. Structs provide validation of the fields when you need it.

While random access in lists is quite slow, random access in maps is O(log n), significantly faster than O(n) for lists. Updating also is O(log n). Whenever possible, any data that you'll heavily edit should be in a map, and data with unique values must be in a map. Maps also work with core Elixir concepts very well, especially pattern matching. Let's see how.

Pattern Matching

Two of the most iconic parts of Elixir, the map datatype and pattern matching, are even stronger in combination. The Elixir community is full of developers who have made the trek from object-oriented programming. Most of them at one time or another try to find a way to replicate inheritance, a way to share behavior across parts of a program. What they are really looking for is polymorphism or a way to write behaviors that work differently for the same data structure. Elixir can simulate polymorphism by explicitly matching map types with pattern matching.

Let's say you have a struct called Animal, like this:

```
defmodule Animal do
  defstruct type: "", legs: 4
end
```

If you wanted to change the implementation of speak based on the type of the animal, it's easy. Within some module you'd do this:

```
def speak(%Animal{type: "dog"}), do: "Woof"
def speak(%Animal{type: "cat"}), do: "Meow"
```

You can also use this technique to delegate speaking to another module altogether.

The difference between this approach and OOP's approach is that you can match on two dimensions at once, say animal.type and animal.size should you need to do so, like this:

```
def speak(%Animal{ type: "dog", size: _}), do: "Woof"
def speak(%Animal{ type: "cat", size: "small"}), do: "Meow"
def speak(%Animal{ type: "cat", size: "large"}), do: "Roar!!!"
```

Inheritance *limits extension to a single dimension.* Often, you may need to be able to invoke logic across more than one dimension. Even if you have thousands of clauses, pattern matching used in this way is *fast*. Matching a map or struct is O(log n).

Another nice feature of pattern matching is quick validation. Say your code expects maps to have a status code set, and if that code is missing, something is broken. If so, you can fail quickly, in the manner of your choosing:

```
def(%{status: status}=thing), do: process(thing)
def(_thing_without_status), do: raise "boom"
```

This strategy allows code that fails quickly and explicitly. Those are the characteristics you want.

We've extolled the virtues of maps, but all languages are opinionated, tempermental beasts. In any language, datatypes work best when they are matched to their intended use. Next we'll look at some traps you'll find as you dive into maps.

Map Traps

These are some of the traps you might fall into if you're not careful. Don't be fooled by the fact that IEx sorts small maps in the console for convenience. You cannot count on this ordering! If you need to enforce order, prefer lists.

Keyword lists were the maps in Elixir before we had true maps. They are literally lists of two-tuples, each with an atom key and any type for a value. They make better function options than maps because they allow duplications and support some useful syntactic sugar. For example, if the last argument in a function is a keyword list, you can omit the surrounding [], such as Elixir's short-form functions.

When you find yourself working with keys and ignoring the values, switch to MapSet. The MapSet is a collection of values of any type that supports ==. They enforce uniqueness and provide a full set of functions for set math. Often, Elixir developers will use maps to enforce uniqueness for things like set math. MapSets are optimized for set math and maps are not. Finally, if you know the keys in advance, you may want to upgrade to a struct. In this book, we'll use structs primarily for *internal interfaces*, except when we're building common infrastructure such as Plug.Conn in the Phoenix framework.

We've just looked at maps and structs. Next are a couple of data structures for dealing with text, charlists, and binaries.

Strings

You've already seen one of our suggestions, to prefer strings for user-defined text and atoms for naming concepts in code. In this section, we're going to dive a little deeper. Elixir's strings have a slightly different set of characteristics from maps or lists, and you should know about those subtle differences. Let's talk a little bit about these concepts.

Elixir has two different kinds of strings. The first is the charlist, and it's just a list of characters, like this:

```
iex> [67, 65, 66]
'CAB'
iex> ?C
67
```

Notice the single quotes. The representation of the charlist is simply a list of numbers, the ASCII codes for those characters. Use this datatype to work with the individual characters in a list, or when you are working with an underlying framework that uses them. You can also use String.graphemes/1 to break a string down into characters.

You may have also noticed strings with double quotes, and they are not the same as charlists:

```
iex> 'CAB' == "CAB"
false
```

The reason is that "CAB" is a compacted string, a more efficient representation. Let's see how.

Strings Are Binaries

Elixir has datatypes and libraries for dealing with strings of data called *bitstrings*. A bitstring that's a multiple of 8 bits is a *binary*. The operator for converting something to a bitstring is << >>. You can actually see them at work, like this:

```
iex> <<?C, ?A, ?B>>
"CAB"
```

The ?C expression returns a code point,[3] the numeric value for "C". That means "?C" is an integer:

```
iex> ?C
67
```

While the <<>> operator looks like a sharp tool that could hurt you, don't be afraid. It's a *binary*, and the most common Elixir strings are binaries manipulated and matched[4] in exactly this way. It's invaluable for storing and

---

3. https://elixir-lang.org/getting-started/binaries-strings-and-char-lists.html
4. https://zohaib.me/binary-pattern-matching-in-elixir/

accessing bytes in a sequence and even breaking them into requisite pieces. As you can see in the following diagram, some elements of strings take one byte and others take two or three:

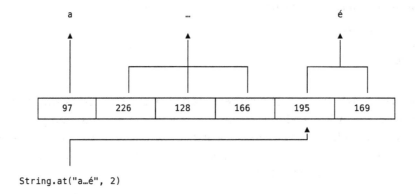

String.at("a…é", 2)

We won't go into more detail, but we encourage you to read more about bit-strings in the Elixir documentation.[5]

For the most part, prefer strings to charlists. They represent data more efficiently. While the mechanics are beyond the scope of this book, you should know binaries are extremely efficient for dealing with low-level protocols. To wrap up this section on strings, we'll look at the common tricks and traps associated with them.

String Traps

Because strings are not typical lists, Elixir has several ways to break the usual rules for efficiency. For example, the BEAM shares long strings across processes,[6] and lets them go after all references are cleared. Therefore, it's extremely important to refrain from letting processes hold references to large strings for longer than needed, to avoid hard-to-find memory leaks.[7] Such leaks can crash the BEAM, and do so in ways that are hard to diagnose.

Keep in mind that editing or even just finding a character are O(n), just as they are with lists. Therefore you shouldn't use long strings to encode information. For example, translating such things as URLs with many parts to an intermediate form can pay big dividends if you're doing many lookups for the component parts, like the protocol, host, path, and query parameters.

---

5.   https://hexdocs.pm/elixir/Kernel.SpecialForms.html#%3C%3C%3E%3E/1

6.   https://medium.com/@mentels/a-short-guide-to-refc-binaries-f13f9029f6e2

7.   https://blog.heroku.com/logplex-down-the-rabbit-hole

For strings, a copy is a full copy, like a tuple instead of a list, but the BEAM cheats as much as it can. To avoid copying strings across processes, if you have a long string, the BEAM puts it into common memory. The BEAM also takes very large strings and cuts them into smaller ones, some of which will never change.

There's another potential trap, string concatenation. Simply put, it's slow. There's a cheat code for this game, though. You should prefer I/O lists to concatenation.[8] That technique is beyond the scope of this book but you can check the footnote to learn more. That's the way that Phoenix templates work, for example. They pass lists of strings to I/O for export instead of concatenating and then processing. That tip makes a huge difference when you're doing high-volume concatenations with large strings.

If your eyes are starting to glaze over, sit tight. There's just a few more datatypes we need to cover, starting with the tuple, before we start to put what we've learned into practice.

Tuples

Tuples are fixed-length data structures. Like all Elixir data structures, they are immutable. You can access, or pattern match against, any element of the tuple and you can do so efficiently. This section will show you the types of problems you can generally solve with tuples.

Good Tuples

Generally, think of tuples as structures where the position within the tuple means something. Coordinates, {key, value} pairs from maps, and {city, state} pairs are all good examples of what you'll see in tuples.

A common and acceptable use for tuples is tagging data. This technique pairs a result tag with data. For example, you'll see this technique in action with many Elixir functions in return codes like {:ok, value} or {:error, reason}

You'll also sometimes find the need to read chunks of data with the same structure, such as columns. These types of rows are data clumps,[9] and APIs that use them favor tuples. Database query results and CSV rows are good examples of data clumps.

---

8.   https://www.bignerdranch.com/blog/elixir-and-io-lists-part-1-building-output-efficiently/

9.   https://refactoring.guru/smells/data-clumps

Tuple Traps

Since tuples are not as structured as other datatypes, they often lead to code that's hard to read or understand. When you find yourself having trouble remembering which element of the tuple goes in which position, it's time to switch to a map. Tuples give no opportunity to label their columns, whether you're matching a particular column or extracting a value from a specific column. This problem is common across many functional languages and it is called connascence of position.[10]

Appending to tuples is slow, as you might expect. You can see in the following figure that appending to a tuple means creating a whole new copy:

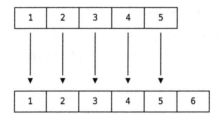

```
Tuple.append({1, 2, 3, 4, 5}, 6)
```

Similarly, if you find yourself editing tuples, you should prefer maps. Tuples are also not enumerable. If you find yourself iterating through them by using an index, switch to a list.

That's most of the Elixir types, but we should offer one more. Let's move on to the most iconic of datatypes for functional languages, the function.

Functions as Data

Since Elixir is a functional language, we should all remember that functions are data too. Sometimes using functions can offer tremendous performance wins.

For example, this is one way to store the drawing instructions for a square:

```
iex(1)> square = [ {:line, {5, 0}, {15, 0}},
                   {:line, {15, 0}, {15, 10}},
                   {:line, {15, 10}, {5, 10}},
                   {:line, {5, 10}, {5, 0}}]
[
  {:line, {5, 0}, {15, 0}},
  {:line, {15, 0}, {15, 10}},
```

---

10. http://connascence.io/position.html

```
  {:line, {15, 10}, {5, 10}},
  {:line, {5, 10}, {5, 0}}
]
```

That way works fine. Each tuple has an instruction, a beginning point and an ending point. A CAD system would have an extensive list of such instructions. The problem comes when you start to partition work across processes. When Elixir moves across process boundaries, it often has to copy data.

Here's another, very powerful, way:

```
iex(2)> square = fn {x, y}, size ->
                [ {:line, {x, y},
                  {x + size, y}},
                  {:line, {x + size, y},
                  {x + size, y + size}},
                  {:line, {x + size, y + size},
                  {x, y + size}},
                  {:line, {x, y + size},
                  {x, y}}
                ]
            end
 #Function<12.127694169/2 in :erl_eval.expr/5>
iex(3)> square.({5, 0}, 10)
[
  {:line, {5, 0}, {15, 0}},
  {:line, {15, 0}, {15, 10}},
  {:line, {15, 10}, {5, 10}},
  {:line, {5, 10}, {5, 0}}
]
```

We start with a function called square. It takes a point and a size, and transforms that data to the same square format we saw earlier. This technique has far-reaching implications for a language built on the actor model[11] with heavy distributed computing influences: don't send the data to the functions because that's slow. Send the functions to the data!

Functions can be sent into processes as part of a message, just like other datatypes. Inside the process, a received function can filter or manipulate data that the code sending the function didn't even have access to. It's also important to remember that these processes could transparently be running on other machines. This can save us from copying a bunch of data across the network. A function can pick out what is needed and then we can copy just that.

---

11. https://www.brianstorti.com/the-actor-model/

When to Leave Elixir

Elixir datatypes are good for many problems, but not all. Data structures built with those types are not always efficient. The classic example is number crunching. If you find yourself working with arrays that you need to update frequently and randomly, you should consider integrating a third-party solution into your program. Such integration strategies are outside the scope of this book, but *Adopting Elixir [Tat18]* has an excellent treatment of techniques you can use.

A great example of when to leave Elixir is a SQL database. Most projects need one and there's so much you can gain from it: ACID compliance, transactions, table joins, and the list goes on for miles. Maybe even more importantly, it's so helpful to be able to scale your database separately from your production Elixir deployment. It's wins all around.

We should point out that the BEAM gives us a toolkit that means we *don't* need external dependencies as often as many other environments do. It's rare to need memcached or Redis for ephemeral state with ets built in. If you need a worker pool or a background job system, you can probably meet your exact need with around 100 lines of code. If you want to save even that, there are libraries that handle the general case for you, without leaving the VM. There are some advantages to having all of this with the rest of your app too: the same data structures work everywhere, you get to use supervision, it's easier to react to subsystems becoming unavailable, and so on. The BEAM is closer to an operating system than most programming language runtimes, so building out various kinds of processing with it is much easier.

This chapter was not long, but the content is dense. It's a good time to take a break and digest what we've consumed so far.

Know Your Elixir Datatypes

In this chapter, we focused on what it means to work with data in the Elixir language. We started with basic datatypes such as atoms and numbers, paying close attention to the traps related to float precision and exhausting the atom table, which can crash the BEAM.

We moved on to lists and maps. For lists, we showed a representation of lists in memory. We emphasize the need to access lists head first. Maps and structs are arguably the workhorses of the language. Access, both read and write, were extremely fast and this datatype is appropriate for a wide list of purposes.

Next, we tackled strings and tuples. We worked through the differences between strings and charlists and practiced accessing elements of a binary. We showed the relative positive usage patterns and traps along the way. We then explored tuples, the fastest data structure for random access but with traps for updating and cognitive load.

We moved on to functions as data. We represented squares as both data and functions. After the original function was built, representing squares with different dimensions was trivial.

Finally, we concluded that Elixir data structures specifically, and functional data structures more broadly, are not appropriate for every problem.

With these tools in our pocket, we can start to write some code. In the next chapter we'll put these tips into practice building the data layer for our quiz project. Let's go!

CHAPTER 3

Start with the Right Data Layer

This chapter will continue looking at the "D" for "data" part of "Do fun things with big, loud worker-bees." We'll use the Elixir datatypes you saw in the previous chapter to roll up data structures. Elixir is a functional programming language and that concept will have a huge impact on how you represent data. In functional programming, functions can't update data in place, they must create new copies that transform data step by step. When your data structures are wrong, your code must compensate and will in turn not only look awkward but also just feel wrong. The following figure shows that your data layer often serves as the foundation:

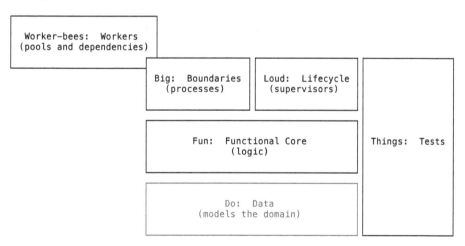

Do fun things with big, loud worker-bees.

In the sections that follow, we'll explore how your foundational data structures will shape your project, especially access patterns. Throughout the chapter, we're going to introduce several different hypothetical problems because we want you to see the impact of data structures on the various decisions we will make.

We'll also explore what it means to build data structures in the functional world, and why it's fundamentally different than programming models like OOP or procedural programming.

Finally, we'll take all of that wisdom and start to design data for a real-world project, a quiz engine. There's a lot on our plate, but it's a tasty dish. Let's get started.

Access Patterns Shape Data Structures

In functional programming, data structures are inextricably linked to functions. Building good programs means considering how those programs use the data. Some data structures are primarily read-only and others exist to be updated. As you saw in the previous chapter, some datatypes are easier to update than others.

Let's take a very simple programming problem, representing a tic-tac-toe game. For those rare folks who have never played this game, it's a childhood favorite where two players, denoted by "X" and "O", take turns putting their markers on a 3x3 grid. The game ends when the first player gets three in a row.

Since it's a small game, performance isn't really a concern. Even when full, our biggest board will have nine cells. We'll be updating the board frequently, and reading frequently as well. Elixir has no multi-dimensional arrays, so we need some kind of composite data structure to represent the game board. Because tuples work best for fixed-length structures, we'll build our board with a three-tuple of three-tuples. Each tuple will have an "X" or "O" for a spot a player has marked, or a " " character for a blank space, like this:

```
iex(1)> board = { {"O", " ", " "},
...(1)>            {" ", "X", " "},
...(1)>            {" ", " ", " "} }
-> {{"O", " ", " "}, {" ", "X", " "}, {" ", " ", " "}}
```

This structure will work. In fact, it has some nice qualities. Accessing random contents is acceptable with pipes and indexes. For example, we can get the middle square like this:

```
iex(2)> board |> elem(1) |> elem(1)
"X"
```

We can even abstract that much into a function, like this:

```
def square(board, row, col) do
  board
  |> elem(row)
  |> elem(col)
end
```

Checking the value of some cell means finding the right row and then finding the right column. Kernel.elem/2 is all we need. square(1, 1) isn't so bad to read, or to use. There's a fly in the ointment though. Things get more complex when we want to change the board. Functional languages are generally immutable, meaning updates return a new copy rather than change the old one. Playing an "X" on the first cell of the middle row looks like this:

```
iex(3)> new_middle_row = board |> elem(1) |> put_elem(0, "X")
{"X", "X", " "}
iex(4)> new_board = put_elem(board, 1, new_middle_row)
{{"O", " ", " "}, {"X", "X", " "}, {" ", " ", " "}}
```

Our data structure is an awkward choice for updates and that awkward structure leads to awkward code. Since the tuples are immutable, *every piece of the data structure that changes* must be replaced. The outer tuple and the middle row need to be changed, and that takes too much awkward code. We need to build a new middle row and place that new middle row into the board. The complexity definitely ramped up when we went from reading to writing. Since our board will probably have only a single update function, the one to make a move, we may be willing to live with this complexity for such a simple game. Still, let's see if we can do better.

Use Cases Shape Data

What if we make one small change by choosing to represent the board as a list of lists of strings?

```
iex(5)> board = [ ["O", " ", " "],
...(5)>           [" ", "X", " "],
...(5)>           [" ", " ", " "] ]
-> [["O", " ", " "], [" ", "X", " "], [" ", " ", " "]]

iex(6)> get_in(board, [Access.at(1), Access.at(1)])
"X"
iex(7)> put_in(board, [Access.at(1), Access.at(0)], "X")
-> [["O", " ", " "], ["X", "X", " "], [" ", " ", " "]]
```

Ah, that's better. We can use Elixir's Access module and paths to update one cell. With this change reading and writing have the same level of complexity. We construct a path into the data structure and hand it to the appropriate function, depending on our intended operation. In fact, the get_in and put_in functions exist exactly because working with nested data structures in Elixir is awkward! A small tweak to how we represent our data has had a noticeable impact on the code that has to manipulate it.

We can do even better, though. One of the problems with both the list of lists and tuple of tuples we chose earlier is the depth, as you will see. Let's explore an alternative.

Prefer Flat Data to Deep Ones

Updates to deep places in data structures are often more complex in deep data structures, as with our tuple of tuples. That's an avoidable problem: don't use deep data structures. In addition, flatter data structures generally allow simpler algorithms and easier pattern matches.

By thinking out of the box, we can get a more effective representation. Maps can use a variety of datatypes as keys, including tuples, like this:

```
iex> board =
... %{
...    {0, 0} => "O", {0, 1} => " ", {0, 2} => " ",
...    {1, 0} => " ", {1, 1} => "X", {1, 2} => " ",
...    {2, 0} => " ", {2, 1} => " ", {2, 2} => " ",
}
```

Now, both reads and writes are trivial:

```
iex> board[{1,1}]
"X"
iex> Map.put(board, {1, 0}, "O")
...
```

Finally, we have a clean, simple way to store and fetch the elements of our board. It's not perfect, though—for instance, the default representation in tools like IEX is ugly. Still, it does allow quick access for storing and retrieving our game pieces.

Here's the moral of our simple example. If you want to write beautiful code, you need to design the right data structures that consider your primary access patterns. This rule of thumb is doubly true for functional languages because data structures are immutable. We'll spend the rest of the chapter giving a little guidance on the *right structure*. We won't give you any silver bullets, but we can offer a few basic rules to help you choose.

At this point, you may be starting to appreciate that working with data in functional programs is different. We've only reached the tip of the iceberg. Read on.

Immutability Drives Everything

You've probably heard that functional programming means that the same inputs will give you the same outputs. You've likely also heard that Elixir binds variables exactly once.

When we say Elixir doesn't allow mutable variables, you might be tempted to push back. Technically, you'd be right, but we should show you the games the compiler is playing to maintain the illusion of mutability. Take a look at this example:

```
iex> x = 10
10
iex> x
10
iex> x = 11
11
iex> x
11
```

That looks like x is mutable, but what you're seeing is not the full picture. The *values* 10 and 11 are immutable. x is a variable that can be rebound at will *within the scope of a function*. Look at this second example:

```
iex> x = 10
10
iex> f = fn() -> x end
#Function<20.99386804/0 in :erl_eval.expr/5>
iex> x = 11
11
iex> x
11
iex> f.()
10
```

Each function has its own bindings and they can't be changed by another function, or another process. In the end, we have immutability. You can't invent a flow that allows colliding mutable values because Erlang, the foundational language, simply doesn't support mutable variables. Once a variable is bound, the underlying representation is fixed, period.

With immutability, rather than updating your data in place, you create a *new* copy of that data. That rule is true of simple types such as integers or complex ones like structs or maps. There are some subtleties related to this approach. Let's look at them.

New Facts Don't Invalidate Old Facts

Sometimes, it helps to think of pieces of data as facts, or assertions about the world. Say you have code that depends on a data structure in a variable in Elixir or some other functional language. Elixir makes a guarantee: that data structure in that variable is always stable. That's why functional languages are so good at concurrency. Multiple processes can access the same data without having to deal with the data changing out from under them.

It does mean that you'll often need to change the way you think about data. In an object-oriented system, a bank account might be an object with a balance and some other fields. The bank account might process transactions at any time, resulting in a changing balance.

On the other hand, a functional bank account is something different entirely. It's an initial balance plus a set of transactions *at a point in time*. These transactions are functions. If you're writing a program, once you have a representation of an account, you don't have to worry about it ever changing. Rather than having an ever-changing account that reflects the present value, you have an account *as of a point in time*. This means that adding new facts doesn't invalidate your old facts. If you're holding an account as of 11:25 and someone makes a deposit at 11:30, you just don't care because your data structure protects you.

Functional programmers look at the world in this way. If you represent a mouse as locations and clicks *at a point in time* rather than a variable (x, y) location that changes over time, each function in your program is dealing with fixed data instead of changing data. Your test cases no longer care about an ever-changing mouse location; an error captured in a log can give you enough information about how to reproduce a problem exactly, and so on.

Object-oriented data structures *change over time*. Functional data structures *are maps of stable values over time*. Functional programs do this automatically. Changing anything means creating a new copy, and your data structures will reflect these new realities. Your programming techniques should reflect this reality.

Write Data Structures Functionally

Let's keep exploring our bank account. Here's one way to think about our bank account example:

```
account:
  %{
    account_number: String,
    account_holder: %User{},
    balance: Int,
    transaction_log: [strings],
  }
```

This structure works OK in many languages, but it is not a functional data structure. There's a hidden problem. Let's take a quick hypothetical.

Processes Are Not Data

Since we're writing an Elixir program, it's tempting to wrap this data in a process, and allow other processes to access it. We have two functions, read_balance and write_balance. Then, say we have other worker processes that use those functions to do the work of debiting and crediting. *Such a design would be a mistake.*

Say two different processes called worker 1 and worker 2 fetch the account balance near the same time, both retrieving a value of say $100. Both wish to modify the balance, one adding $50 and one subtracting $50. They then both write their balance, as in the following figure. Depending on which actor writes first, the balance will be either $50 or $150. Both are incorrect. Either the bank or the user will be happy, for a while, but the data is inconsistent with the truth.

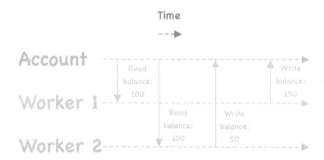

What we've done is built our own datatype with processes, with its own set of rules. We've taken much of the goodness of functional programming away. We have built something that works just like an OOP variable that answers the question "What is the current balance?"

A much better question is "What is the balance at a specific time?" To answer that question, we can store an initial balance and all of the *changes* represented in our transactions. We can get all transactions since the beginning of time, or if this becomes a performance problem, all transactions since a checkpoint. We're never changing the initial balance. We're just adding transactions to our account as they come in, like this:

```
account:
  %{
    account_number: String,
    initial_balance: Integer,
    account_holder: %User{},
    transactions: [%Transaction{}],
  }

transaction:
  %{
    change: Integer,
    inserted_at: DateTime,
    note: String,
  %}
```

```
def balance(account_number, date_time), do: ...
```

Hey, we know these aren't true type specs, but bear with us. We're trying to communicate abstract concepts instead of precise types.

In this example, balance becomes a *function* that computes a balance at a point in time based on adding all of the *transactions*, each with a change that has positive or negative values. We can then start with a balance and reduce over the transactions to get a balance. There's no ambiguity. It's completely deterministic.

To get the most out of functional programming, you're going to have to extend the thinking beyond the *functions* and into the *data*. With these high-level concepts in mind, it's time to dive to a lower level and look at data in Elixir itself.

Try It Out

Let's take the ideas we've learned and put them into practice. Throughout the rest of the book, we're going to build a project that generates quizzes. As a rough rule of thumb, we'll start by thinking about the nouns in the system. Those will be data, and many of them will be custom datatypes.

Let's get started. From a system console, create a new mix project:

```
mix new mastery --sup
```

That command creates a new project. We added the --sup flag because we'll be building an OTP project and it will need a supervisor. We'll need to fill the project with a few data structures, but as usual, it pays to think first.

Break Nouns into Data Structures

In our *quiz* project, we can have *templates* in various *categories* that create *questions*. For an example, a template for a simple addition problem may be <%= left %> + <%= right %> with [0, 1, 2, 3, 4, 5, 6, 7, 8, 9] being valid values for left and right. This means a quiz might generate 3 + 2 or 0 + 0. As we ask questions, we track the *user's responses* and we keep generating questions until our user masters the template. Once they get three in a row right, we'll let them move on to the next category. Look at the following figure for a quick overview of the data layer:

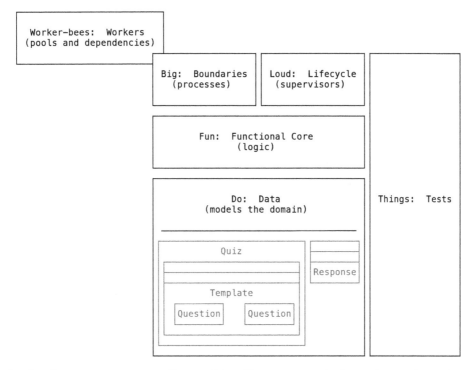

In this figure, you can see that picking the nouns out of our description gives us a good start toward the structure of our data. A *category* will be a string, and a *user* will just be an email address for now. The rest of those nouns—quizzes, templates, questions, and responses—are going to be structs in our system. Let's take a look.

Define a Template

We're going to use the primary Elixir data structure, the map. We know exactly what the fields will be and that's a struct. The centerpiece of our *quiz* is the template. The fields in our templates will serve three purposes.

Our Flow

In truth, when we wrote this code, we didn't magically land on the perfect data structure. We made mistakes, refactored our data, refactored our functions, and then made more mistakes. We're showing you all of these data structures in their final form because we think it makes a better book, one that reinforces our layering concepts.

Our first three fields will describe our templates. As such, we'll have a name and a category, which we'll represent as atoms. We'll also have an instruction to tell users what to do as they answer a question. These are the fields that describe our template:

name (atom)
    The name of this template.

category (atom)
    A grouping for questions of the same name.

instructions (string)
    A string telling the user how to answer questions of this type.

Second, our templates will generate questions. We'll need the raw and compiled version of the template to generate a question, and a generator for each substitution pattern in our template. These are the fields that support question generation:

raw (string)
    The template code before compilation.

compiled (macro)
    The compiled version of the template for execution.

generators (%{ substitution: list or function})
    The generator for each substitution in a template. Each generator is a list of elements or a function. Generating a template substitution will either fire the function or pick a random item from the list.

Finally, our templates will check responses. This responsibility will fall on the checkers, which are functions. This is the field for processing responses:

checker (function(substitutions, string) -> boolean)
    Given the substitutions strings and an answer, the function returns true if the answer is correct. For example, fn subs, answer -> to_string(subs.left + subs.right) == String.trim(answer) end).

Taken together, we have a structure that defines the template. We'll create a lib/mastery/core directory to hold the modules with our data layer (and later our core functions). Crack open lib/mastery/core/template.ex and key this in:

```
defmodule Mastery.Core.Template do
  defstruct ~w[name category instructions raw compiled generators checker]a
end
```

We use the sigil ~w to create a list of words. Though you usually see () characters with this sigil, the [] characters work perfectly fine. The a modifier means the statement will create a list of atoms instead of strings. This data structure is complex, but it reflects the values we've discussed in this section. Rather than just keeping transient data, this permanent data structure gives us everything we need. We can use the data structure to:

- Represent a grouping of questions on a quiz
- Generate questions with a compilable template and functions
- Check the response of a single question in the template

We have the data for a template. Now we can move on to the individual questions.

Templates Generate Questions

Once again, we have a known set of fields of disparate types. That structure screams map. Questions consist of the text a user is asked, the template that created them, and the specific substitutions used to build this question. These are the field details:

asked (String.t)

The question text for a user. For example, "1 + 2".

template (Template.t)

The template that created the question.

substitutions (%{ substitution: any})

The values chosen for each substitution field in a template. For example, for a template <%= left %> + <%= right %>, the substitutions might be %{ "left" => 1, "right" => 2}.

Templates generate questions, and questions are instantiations of those templates. Once again the data structure is functional. A question is immutable and constant. Now, let's code it up. Create a new file called lib/mastery/core/question.ex and make it look like this:

```
defmodule Mastery.Core.Question do
  defstruct ~w[asked substitutions template]a
end
```

Those are the three fields we need: the asked question, the actual substitutions for this question, and the template we used to create this one. Now that we have the templates and questions, we should allow a user to answer a question.

Users Answer with Responses

When a user answers a question, we'll generate a response. Our responses don't really need too much data. We'll track some extra data we might have otherwise computed just to make it easy to debug and reason about the program. This is the data we want to track:

quiz_title (String.t)
  Title field from the quiz.

template_name (atom)
  Name field identifying the template.

to (String.t)
  The question being answered, as in "this is a response *to* the asked question."

email (String.t)
  The email address of the user answering the question.

answer (String.t)
  The answer provided by the user.

correct (boolean)
  Whether the given answer was correct.

timestamp (Time.t)
  The time the answer was provided.

The code to implement those fields is, as you might expect, a struct. Create a new lib/mastery/core/response.ex to look like this:

```
defmodule Mastery.Core.Response do
  defstruct ~w[quiz_title template_name to email answer correct timestamp]a
end
```

That's all we really need. We could have provided the underlying question and quiz, but since we'll be dealing with many responses, it's nice to be able to print them cleanly, and keep these data structures flat. Next, we roll it all together in a quiz.

Quizzes Ask Questions

Here's one of the key concepts of Mastery. Our quiz will ask questions until a user achieves mastery. Once we have templates that create questions, we can use them to build quizzes. Before we code up this data structure, let's talk about our overall strategy.

We'll start with a set of templates, organized by category. We'll cycle through the templates, one at a time. Once the user gets enough right in a row, we'll stop asking that question.

Given that set of directions, we'll need to keep track of the following.

For the overall quiz, we'll need to name the quiz, and we'll need to let the user specify how many answers a user will need to get correct before we finish asking the question:

title (String.t)
> The title for a quiz.

mastery (integer)
> The number of questions a user must get right to master a quiz category.

Next, we'll need to keep track of some metadata as users advance through the quiz:

current_question (Question.t)
> The current question being presented to the user.

last_response (Response.t)
> The last response given by the user.

templates (%{ "category" => [Template.t]})
> The master list of templates, by category.

used ([Template.t])
> The templates that we've used, this cycle, that have not yet been mastered.

mastered ([Template.t])
> The templates that have been mastered.

record (%{ "template_name" => integer})
> The number of correct answers in a row a user has given for each template.

That's all we need. With the fields we need, let's build a struct with the fields and defaults we'll need. Crack open lib/mastery/core/quiz.ex and make it look like this:

```elixir
defmodule Mastery.Core.Quiz do
  defstruct title: nil,
            mastery: 3,
            templates: %{ },
            used: [ ],
            current_question: nil,
            last_response: nil,
            record: %{ },
            mastered: [ ]
end
```

Initially, all questions will start in templates. The quiz will select a question, and that question will move from templates to used. After all questions get asked once, unless they're mastered in the meantime, they'll move back from used to templates.

Getting an answer right will increment a record, and getting enough right in a row will move a template from used to mastered. Getting an answer wrong will reset the record.

We haven't written any code yet, but we have a pretty good idea of how our program will work, just by looking at the data structure of the quiz. We know the overall structure our component will take. We have a good idea how our algorithms will work as we create templates, add them to a quiz, and then move from question to question. The representation of our data will drive how we think about managing the quiz.

We are not yet thinking about the user interface or database layers at all. We'll address those concerns elsewhere. Our next job is to create the functional core that will manipulate those data structures.

That's enough to digest. It's time to wrap up.

Start with the Right Data

First, we examined how choices of data structure might change access patterns and impact the complexity of the code we write. We introduced simple principles to keep data structures flat and saw that functional data structures are generally slower.

Next we introduced the way functional programmers shape data, preferring many versions of a value over time rather than continuously mutating a single value.

We looked at Elixir's data structures, including lists, tuples, maps, and structs, among others. We showed some of the strengths and weaknesses of each.

Finally, we applied all of those lessons using a functional component. We defined templates with functions to generate questions, and we defined function fields to check each question we created. When we were done, we had a rough skeleton to build on.

In the next chapter, we'll begin to add meat to those bones. We'll build a functional core to manipulate the data structures, functions that will create questions from templates, check responses, and move the quiz from question to question as the user answers them. We'll build a concise layer that will be easy to reason about and easy to test before we get into the intricacies of concurrency and state.

It's starting to get exciting. Turn the page and let's write some functions.

CHAPTER 4

Build a Functional Core

In this chapter, we'll dive into the functional core, sometimes called the business logic of your component. Functional-core is the "F" for "fun" in "Do fun things with big loud worker-bees." In the previous chapter, we worked with data. We carved our project into hollow modules holding structs that form our data skeleton. In this chapter, we'll fill those empty modules up with functions, each logically addressing a part of the whole functional core. The following figure shows where this core fits:

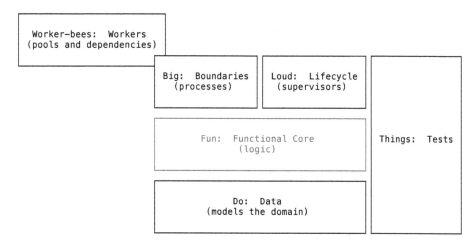

Do fun things with big, loud worker-bees.

A functional core is a group of functions and the type definitions representing the data layer, organized into modules. Our core doesn't access external interfaces or use any process machinery your component might use. In Elixir, that process machinery is the GenServer, and those bits are banished to the outer bands of our architecture.

Your core will present a clear, stable interface to any external code. This API decouples core code from any process machinery in the outer layers and hides implementation details. By establishing a firm API without side effects to the rest of the world, you can effectively deal with your most complex code piece by piece. Your algorithm complexity and process machinery are defined in isolated layers so you can deal with each separately. In the end, each piece is easier to test and understand so the whole is more manageable.

Just as your data shapes your functions, your functional core will shape your tests, your boundary layer, and ultimately the code your clients write. The most understandable Elixir code uses composition features to weave functions together into an easily understandable story, and your core will lean on those composition features heavily.

Some say that functional cores should be pure functions. In this book, we won't say too much about "pure" versus "impure" functions because such debates are rarely constructive. We do think it's important to mention the concept of purity here. For the most part, a pure function returns the same value given the same inputs each time you run it.

Your core doesn't have to be completely pure. Some functions will have concepts like timestamps, ID generation, or random number generation that are not strictly pure. For the most part, though, a functional core gets much easier to manage if the same inputs always generate the same outputs.

As we build our quiz project, the functional core will use a random number generator because that's where we believe that concept should be. As we write test cases, you'll see that we pay the price for making that compromise.

In the sections that follow, we're going to build our functional core for our Mastery project. As we walk through each module, we'll illustrate some core concepts of composing with functions along the way. When we're done you'll have a better understanding of how cores work. You'll also know some useful techniques for weaving together those functions inside the core.

Organize Core Functions by Purpose

Recall our initial data architecture. We have Quizzes made up of Templates and Questions. Users answer questions with Responses. We designed our data by putting structs inside empty modules. That design will serve as a useful foundation of our core, as shown in the figure on page 55.

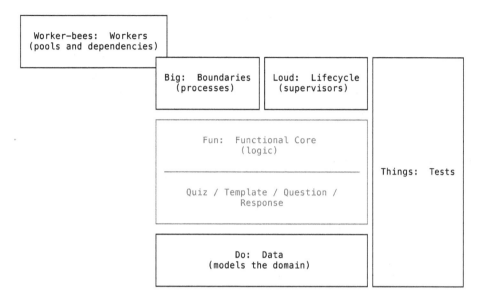

Now, we'll slowly start to fill those modules up with functions. It's time to build out the first few modules for our Quiz component.

Let's look first at three pieces of our Mastery core: the Response, Question, and Template. Remember, each of these is a module, and also the name of the struct that lives inside the module. We will fill each of those modules with functions that deal with those structs.

This is a primary Elixir design goal. When you group like functions together based on the data with the sole purpose of managing that kind of data, Elixir code becomes easier to code. You'll find that it's easier to compose with pipes and easier to tell where functions belong.

Let's start with a simple example. Nothing in Mastery is simpler than a Response.

You might wonder how large a module has to be. The answer is "as big as it needs to be to do a single job." On a module basis, we want to keep the external API simple and internal details hidden. That way the interactions between modules will be simpler. In a sense, we're building layers inside of layers.

Some of our modules have only data and a constructor, and that's OK. Responses exist only to be data-holding structs, so all we need is a constructor. Think of a constructor as a convenience function to instantiate a piece of data. Add your constructor to lib/mastery/core/response.ex, like this:

Code Structure

The example code for this book will be packaged by chapter. You'll see a filename at the top that will point you to the folder for the chapter, and then the project code therein. For example, the code in this chapter will live in FunctionsCore with the code in FunctionsCore/lib and the tests in FunctionsCore/test.

FunctionsCore/lib/mastery/core/response.ex
```elixir
defmodule Mastery.Core.Response do
  defstruct ~w[quiz_title template_name to email answer correct timestamp]a

  def new(quiz, email, answer) do
    question = quiz.current_question
    template = question.template

    %__MODULE__{
      quiz_title: quiz.title,
      template_name: template.name,
      to: question.asked,
      email: email,
      answer: answer,
      correct: template.checker.(question.substitutions, answer),
      timestamp: DateTime.utc_now
    }
  end
end
```

We're using __MODULE__ instead of typing the full name of the module because that code defaults to the current module, and protects us from refactoring code whenever we reorganize the project.

If you were designing your own Mastery component, you might be tempted to put questions and templates together, but we chose not to do so because *templates* and *questions* are different concepts with different purposes. A template exists to generate questions, and a question exists to present an answerable construct to a user.

Edit to a Single Purpose

We're approaching the first complex piece of our project, the template. After all, templates will need to compile code to perform substitutions. You may find it tempting to reach right for a GenServer instead of pure functions to build our template. If we did that, we'd need to take another pass through our design since we're working only with modules within our functional core, and cores don't deal with processes.

When you run into situations like this one, we'd like to counsel you to sit tight and try to attack the problem with functions first, and those should be as pure as you can make them. Our rule of thumb is to use processes only when we need them to control execution, divide work, or store common state where functions won't work.

Given that rule of thumb, we'll try to keep things inside the core by carving our modules into specific functions. If we hit a wall and find a problem that mandates a task or a GenServer, we'll slow down and re-examine our interfaces. For now, recall the struct defining the data for templates:

```
defstruct ~w[name category instructions raw compiled generators checker]a
```

The templates have some descriptive names, but the most important pieces are the raw field containing code we're going to use to create questions, generators to fill in each of the substitutions in the template, and a checker functions to test results. For now, let's focus on the raw field. The rest will come into play when we write tests, generate quizzes, and answer questions.

A typical template for a math problem might be <%= left %> + <%= right %>. We'll compile that to Elixir, and put the result in compiled. We'll need to compile templates as users create them. That's a library function, not a process function so it belongs in our core. Open up the existing lib/mastery/core/template.ex and add the new function:

```
FunctionsCore/lib/mastery/core/template.ex
defmodule Mastery.Core.Template do
  defstruct ~w[name category instructions raw compiled generators checker]a

  def new(fields) do
    raw = Keyword.fetch!(fields, :raw)
    struct!(
      __MODULE__,
      Keyword.put(fields, :compiled, EEx.compile_string(raw))
    )
  end
end
```

Typically, we'll create a simple constructor named new when we want to add any default behaviors to the default constructor for struct. Since struct! takes some fields as a Keyword, we'll conform to that API. We'll compile the template and add it to the keyword list.

EEx is a module used to compile idiomatic Elixir templates, called EEx templates. Though our template looked complex on the surface, it wraps the complexity in the EEx module, and that module does the work in a reasonably pure way.

There's no need for a GenServer because we can use pure functions instead. Much of the time, solutions with functions can satisfy many of our needs.

Now we can use those templates to create questions. Let's strategize a bit. Recall that our question fields look like this:

```
defstruct ~w[asked substitutions template]a
```

We will need to use the template to generate the question text we put in asked, and we'll store the template we use to generate a question, as well as the substitutions we choose. Note that we can't really compute asked because sometimes we're going to rely on a function to pick a random substitution from a list, and we want the question to be locked down once we decide to ask a user.

Since we'll need templates to create questions, let's add an alias to make it easier. Open up lib/mastery/core/question.ex to add this code:

FunctionsCore/lib/mastery/core/question.ex
```
defmodule Mastery.Core.Question do
  alias Mastery.Core.Template

  defstruct ~w[asked substitutions template]a
```

These are the things a question needs to be able to do:

- We need a constructor called new that will take a Template and generate a Question.

- We need a function to build the substitutions to plug into our templates.

- As we build substitutions, we'll need to process two different kinds of generators, a random choice from a list and a function that generates a substitution.

- We need to process the substitutions for our template.

Let's start from the bottom up. We need to generate substitutions. We'll use those substitution strings to fill out our template. Recall that our template had generators. We have two types of generators, a list of potential substitutions or a function. If it's a function, we'll execute it; if it's a list, we'll pick a random element from it, like this:

FunctionsCore/lib/mastery/core/question.ex
```
defp build_substitution({name, choices_or_generator}) do
  {name, choose(choices_or_generator)}
end
```

```
defp choose(choices) when is_list(choices) do
  Enum.random(choices)
end

defp choose(generator) when is_function(generator) do
  generator.()
end
```

The magic happens in the choose function supporting build_substitution. choose matches each of our generator types and picks the appropriate one. If it's a generator, we call it; if it's a list, we pick a random one with Enum.random. Then the build_substitution function takes a two-tuple with a name and a generator and returns a tuple with a two-tuple having a name and substitution.

Functions Are Data

The generators in the previous example illustrate an underappreciated aspect of functional programming: functions are just another datatype. Anywhere you can pass some data as an argument, you can pass a function instead. The BEAM even serializes functions, just like other types.

When you learn to think of functions as data, it should radically change the way you approach problems. Take another look at the previous example. We wrapped the template.generator functions with choose/1 to normalize our treatment of options. We combined this tool with guard functions so choose becomes a general tool that works with both lists and functions. That code greatly simplifies the build_substitution function to a trivial level.

Elixir and Erlang use functions as data all over the place, to process random numbers and manage iterators and streams. They take functions that produce the next values. The entire OTP is based on *behaviours* that use groups of functions to implement common patterns. The list goes on and on.

Joe Armstrong, one of the creators of Erlang, used to say we're always taking the data to the code, which is really hard, when we could take the code to the data, and that's much easier. In Elixir, this idea is tremendously powerful.

Name Concepts with Functions

Sometimes, when we have a concept in our code that needs a description, it's tempting to reach for a comment. Instead, think about whether there's a way to name the concept with code. A new variable or a function with a descriptive name is better than a comment because those concepts get checked by the compiler and comments don't. Let's look at an example.

In the first version of this code, we combined the concepts of compiling a macro and evaluating it in a single function that looked like this:

```
defp evaluate(substitutions, template) do
{asked, _bound} =
  Code.eval_quoted(template.compiled, assigns: substitutions)

  %__MODULE__{
    asked: asked,
    substitutions: substitutions,
    template: template
  }
end
```

After thinking about it more, we opted to simplify that code by following two coding principles. The first is single-purpose functions. The second is using functions to name important concepts. We decided to break out the compilation concept. That led to a better design. Given substitutions and a template, let's fill in the template to form our question text. Crack open lib/mastery/core/question.ex and add these functions:

FunctionsCore/lib/mastery/core/question.ex

```
  defp compile(template, substitutions) do
    template.compiled
    |> Code.eval_quoted(assigns: substitutions)
    |> elem(0)
  end

  defp evaluate(substitutions, template) do
    %__MODULE__{
      asked: compile(template, substitutions),
      substitutions: substitutions,
      template: template
    }
  end
end
```

We named the compile concept with a function called compile to do the work, we pipe template.compiled to Code.eval_quoted which returns a tuple. We need the first element, so we grab that with elem(0) and we're off to the races. Now that we can build substitutions and evaluate the template, it's trivial to build our remaining constructor, called new. Key these lines into the top of the module, just below the struct:

FunctionsCore/lib/mastery/core/question.ex

```
def new(%Template{ } = template) do
  template.generators
  |> Enum.map(&build_substitution/1)
  |> evaluate(template)
end
```

We have a good start in our organization. We've defined functions for the simple modules in our system, Response, Question, and Template. We've chosen a problem with meat on it for a reason, though.

Organizing the quiz will stretch us a little more. Let's explore some of the basic principles of functional programming and put those into practice as we compose the functions that make up our quiz.

Compose a Quiz from Functions

Every program is a conversation; as programmers, our first job is to be understood. Whether you're communicating to your future teammate or future you, the goals should be the same. This section is about writing functions that are easier to understand. Though getting better at this critical skill is a lifelong pursuit, adding certain tools to your tool belt where you can use them daily will improve your readability immediately, if you're not already using them.

Hopefully, we'll give terminology and voice to concepts you've already experienced. Over the next few sections, watch for some important concepts as we write code. We will choose function names to fully communicate core concepts. Those well-named functions will focus on a single purpose. Then, we'll structure those functions specifically for composition.

Build Well-Named Functions

If a program is a story, functions represent the verbs, a critical part of your vocabulary. Your function arguments are nouns. Programming is about naming things well. Too many programmers are afraid of long names. Usually, that's a mistake. The best name is *as long as it needs to be.* Consider this example:

```
def tax(amount, city, state, sku), do: ...
```

That name may save typing, but it carries a pretty significant risk because it does not have enough information. It needs context. We could make the name more descriptive, and it would help:

```
def compute_cart_tax(amount, city, state, sku), do: ...
```

Now we know the tax is for a shopping cart. We have more context and less of a chance of confusion that could change business behavior. Still, an important piece of information is missing:

```
def compute_cart_tax_in_cents(taxable_cents, city, state, sku), do: ...
```

Now we're getting there. cart shows what we're computing, and in_cents makes sure our clients know we're returning currency in cents rather than dollars. If you're so inclined, you could use a typespec and explicitly specify dollars and cent types to accomplish the same things.

To be fair, short names have their place. Honk if you'd rather be typing Enumerable than Enum. For the most part, though, acronyms and abbreviations do more harm than good. Functions are opportunities to name concepts. Take full advantage.

Shape Them for Composition

Once you have functions with good names, the next step in organizing them is to shape them for composition. In Elixir, that means pipes. The progression of good Elixir code often goes something like this:

- Try to string together a pipeline of transformations using |>.
- Fallback to with/1 when you need to embrace failure.
- To shape code that's difficult to compose, use tokens (more on this later).

In Elixir, we'll typically want to compose across functions with these strategies. In the core, we'll focus on the first and third concepts, both forms of piping. In the service layer, we'll lean on the second, since we'll have to deal with more failure and uncertainty, places where with shines.

So far, we've built out questions, templates, and responses. With modules having functions shaped around a single concept and taking a common datatype as the first argument, we're already moving toward structures that will pipe well. When functions in your module also return the module's struct, you're built to pipe. Then complex multipurpose functions break down into pipes of single-purpose functions.

The concept we mention above, tokens, is an extreme form of composition with pipes. Let's explore.

Use Tokens to Share Complex Context

One of the key concepts in functional programming is the token.[1] Think of a token as a piece representing a player on a board game. It moves and marks concepts. Tokens in programming are very much the same.

If you're familiar with the Phoenix framework, the Plug.Conn is a token. An Ecto.Changeset or Query is also a token. Pipelines of functions transform these structures, tracking progress through a program.

Think about our quiz. The quiz will mark a user's progress through answering a set of generated questions as they master concepts and repeat others. It's not a linear progression through a list, or a reduction across some other datatype. It's a token, the representation of a quiz at a point in time. Our quiz is still a functional data structure because we represent each point in time with a different quiz.

Build Single-Purpose Functions

Let's use these concepts to build out our quiz. Along the way we can examine other principles of good design. We'll try to make each function take on one single task, however simple. Functions should be relatively short, but a much more important concept is to keep them to a single task. Decoupling concepts is a foundational concept for any kind of programming, regardless of language.

Let's put this advice into practice as we build our quiz. Recall our initial structure for quizzes (Quizzes Ask Questions, on page 49). We have the struct, the constructor, and the common aliases we'll need to keep our sanity and reduce our typing. Open up lib/mastery/core/quiz.ex and key this in:

```
FunctionsCore/lib/mastery/core/quiz.ex
defmodule Mastery.Core.Quiz do
  alias Mastery.Core.{Template, Question, Response}

  defstruct title: nil,
            mastery: 3,
            templates: %{ },
            used: [ ],
            current_question: nil,
            last_response: nil,
            record: %{ },
            mastered: [ ]

  def new(fields) do
    struct!(__MODULE__, fields)
  end
end
```

Sometimes we don't need to build a custom constructor, but in this case, the new function will help us compose cleanly in our tests and other functions.

Our next few functions allow us to add a template to the quiz. Remember, our Quiz is a token. It will track the composition of new quizzes and track a user through answering questions. Building a single-purpose function to add templates to a quiz makes sense:

FunctionsCore/lib/mastery/core/quiz.ex

```
def add_template(quiz, fields) do
  template = Template.new(fields)

  templates =
    update_in(
      quiz.templates,
      [template.category],
      &add_to_list_or_nil(&1, template)
    )

  %{quiz | templates: templates}
end

defp add_to_list_or_nil(nil, template), do: [template]
defp add_to_list_or_nil(templates, template), do: [template | templates]
```

Here we create a new template and add it to quiz.templates[category], building a new list if none exists and returning a new module. That means when it's time, we can beautifully generate a new test like this:

```
Quiz.new(title: "Basic math", mastery: 4)
|> add_template(fields_for_addition)
|> add_template(fields_for_subtraction)
|> add_template(fields_for_multiplication)
|> add_template(fields_for_division)
```

Each step moves our token with a simple transformation. Each step represents a single-purpose function, and we compose each of those to form bigger steps. Once the quiz has templates, we're ready to pick a question for the user. Let's do that now.

Build at a Single Level of Abstraction

As we're building the quiz, we'll continue to build single-purpose functions that are easy to compose. One of the things that makes code easy or hard to read is the number of abstractions a programmer has to deal with at once. It turns out that we can handle many different abstractions if those abstractions are well named, well organized, and close together. This concept is the single level of abstraction[2] principle introduced by Bob Martin in *Clean Code: A Handbook of Agile Software Craftsmanship [Mar08]*.

Choose a Random Question

The single level of abstraction principle says that each line of a function or method should be at the same level of abstraction. It's a tough principle to

---

2. http://principles-wiki.net/principles:single_level_of_abstraction

articulate, but we know it when we see it. A good example of that principle is our select_question function:

```
FunctionsCore/lib/mastery/core/quiz.ex
def select_question(%__MODULE__{templates: t}) when map_size(t) == 0, do: nil
def select_question(quiz) do
  quiz
  |> pick_current_question
  |> move_template(:used)
  |> reset_template_cycle
end
```

That code is written to a single level of abstraction. It picks a random question, moves the template to the used list, and resets the cycle if we've gone through all of our templates.

Earlier versions of our code looked like this:

```
def select_question(quiz) do
  quiz
  |> Map.put( :current_question, select_a_random_question(quiz) )
  |> move_template(:used)
  |> reset_template_cycle
end
```

The problem is that Map.put is at a different level of abstraction than select_a_question. One deals with questions; one deals with Elixir basic datatypes. Sometimes, code written to a single level of abstraction is longer. In the end, it's worth it because the most complex logic is what we're optimizing. Let's fill out the details of selecting a question by looking at each of the individual pieces. First, we'll look at pick_current_question:

```
FunctionsCore/lib/mastery/core/quiz.ex
defp pick_current_question(quiz) do
  Map.put(
    quiz,
    :current_question,
    select_a_random_question(quiz)
  )
end

defp select_a_random_question(quiz) do
  quiz.templates
  |> Enum.random
  |> elem(1)
  |> Enum.random
  |> Question.new
end
```

Recall that quiz templates has a list of all unused templates for a test, grouped by category. The function select_a_random_question takes a random template category in the form {category_name, templates}, selects the second element of the tuple at index 1, picks a random template from that list, and then creates a new question based on that template.

Then pick_current_question adds that question to a quiz. pick_current_question exists solely to make select_a_random_question composable by returning a Quiz, which is our token.

Move Our Tokens Through Transformations

Remember, our quiz is a token, like a token on a game board. Think of our token advancing through the game board squares where each square is a new question. The most critical advancements happen when we choose a question and when the user answers questions. The Quiz token will need to seamlessly move through states just as a token moves through the game.

With a question chosen, we can now move a template from our master quiz.templates list to quiz.used, like this:

FunctionsCore/lib/mastery/core/quiz.ex
```
defp move_template(quiz, field) do
  quiz
  |> remove_template_from_category
  |> add_template_to_field(field)
end

defp template(quiz), do: quiz.current_question.template
```

Moving a template to used or any other field is the same, so we generalize the concept. We remove the template from the quiz.templates list and then add it to the specified field of quiz. We'll get to the details next, but first we'll define a helper function to make things a little easier.

The current *template* for a quiz comes from the current *question* for a quiz, so we have a simple helper function called quiz.template that returns the template from the current question.

Let's look at that remove_template_from_category function now:

FunctionsCore/lib/mastery/core/quiz.ex
```
defp remove_template_from_category(quiz) do
  template = template(quiz)
  new_category_templates =
    quiz.templates
    |> Map.fetch!(template.category)
    |> List.delete(template)
```

```
  new_templates =
    if new_category_templates == [ ] do
      Map.delete(quiz.templates, template.category)
    else
      Map.put(quiz.templates, template.category, new_category_templates)
    end

  Map.put(quiz, :templates, new_templates)
end
```

This function is a little awkward because it deals with the most complex of our data structures in a quiz, the path quiz.templates[category]. We start by computing the new value for quiz.templates. We get templates[category] and then delete the current template from the list.

Next, we build the new quiz.templates record. This is made slightly more complicated because we don't want an empty category, so if the new list of templates for a category is empty, we delete the key in quiz.templates. Otherwise, we put the new template list into quiz.templates[category].

This code isn't complex but it is awkward. We hide the complexity from the user by wrapping it in a single-purpose function. The only time a coder needs to consider this code is when they are reprogramming how templates are organized.

Now that we've done the hard part, we can move on to happier things. Adding our template to a field is as simple as Map.put, like this:

FunctionsCore/lib/mastery/core/quiz.ex
```
defp add_template_to_field(quiz, field) do
  template = template(quiz)
  list = Map.get(quiz, field)

  Map.put(quiz, field, [template | list])
end
```

We get the current template, we get the list for the field, and then replace that list with a new list having our new template.

Reset a Quiz

After we've moved all of the templates from quiz.templates to quiz.used, we need to consider what to do next, now that quiz.templates is empty. If the quiz user has yet to master all concepts in the quiz, we need to reset quiz.templates from the quizzes we've used but not yet mastered. That will happen in reset_template_cycle, like this:

```
FunctionsCore/lib/mastery/core/quiz.ex
defp reset_template_cycle(%{templates: templates, used: used} = quiz)
when map_size(templates) == 0 do
  %__MODULE__{
    quiz |
    templates: Enum.group_by(used, fn template -> template.category end),
    used: [ ]
  }
end
defp reset_template_cycle(quiz), do: quiz
```

Now, our token can successfully represent new quizzes, adding templates to quizzes, and advancing through questions. The next step is to finish up our business logic by letting a user answer questions.

Keep the Left Margin Skinny

You can tell a lot about a programmer by scanning code. For Elixir, this is especially true. When scanning Elixir, look for long pipelines, short functions, and skinny left margins. We've talked about designing for composition and single level of abstraction. Skinny left margins mean decisions are often made in pattern matches instead of control structures like if, cond, and case. Skinny left margins make single concept functions much more likely, and simplify tests. Let's take an example.

When a user answers a question, the response may be correct or incorrect. We've built a boolean into our Response struct for the purposes of quickly making decisions with pattern matching. It looks like this:

```
FunctionsCore/lib/mastery/core/quiz.ex
def answer_question(quiz, %Response{correct: true}=response) do
  new_quiz =
    quiz
    |> inc_record
    |> save_response(response)
  maybe_advance(new_quiz, mastered?(new_quiz))
end
def answer_question(quiz, %Response{correct: false}=response) do
  quiz
  |> reset_record
  |> save_response(response)
end

def save_response(quiz, response) do
  Map.put(quiz, :last_response, response)
end
```

```
def mastered?(quiz) do
  score = Map.get(quiz.record, template(quiz).name, 0)
  score == quiz.mastery
end
```

We decide how to handle a response by pattern matching on response.correct. When we answer a question, the behavior is different for correct and incorrect questions. In either case, we need to appropriately set the number of consecutive correct answers which we store in quiz.record and to save the response in quiz.last_response.

If the answer is correct, we increment the record, save the response, and may possibly advance, based on whether the user has mastered that template. We'll handle the potential advancement in maybe_advance. On an incorrect response, we reset the record for that template and save the response.

The save_response function is just a Map.put. We break out a function only to name the concept. Similarly, mastered? is trivial. A template is mastered? if the record matches the quiz mastery.

This coding style may seem alien to you at first, but once you get used to it, reading code like this is more like reading independent business rules, and flows seamlessly. Debugging is often simpler because you'll often have the arguments to a failing function when things break, so you have all the data you need at your disposal.

Let's look at the independent pieces that make up answer_question. For a right answer, we need to increment the record, like this:

FunctionsCore/lib/mastery/core/quiz.ex
```
defp inc_record(%{current_question: question}=quiz) do
  new_record = Map.update(quiz.record, question.template.name, 1, &(&1 + 1))
  Map.put(quiz, :record, new_record)
end
```

Easy. We compute the new record with Map.update. That function takes a data structure, a path to data within that structure, a default value and a function. The function updates the data at the path with the given function, using the default if there's not yet a value.

Next, we handle advancing. This is the crux of our token movement, but breaking our system down into composable steps makes quick work of it:

FunctionsCore/lib/mastery/core/quiz.ex
```
defp maybe_advance(quiz, false = _mastered), do: quiz
defp maybe_advance(quiz, true = _mastered), do: advance(quiz)
```

```
def advance(quiz) do
  quiz
  |> move_template(:mastered)
  |> reset_record
  |> reset_used
end
```

Notice we name the second boolean argument, and immediately discard that name. We're doing so to name the concept related to the boolean as _mastered. If a concept is not yet mastered, we do nothing, meaning we return our token, the quiz. Once a concept is mastered, we move the template to quiz.mastered, reset quiz.record for that category to zero, and reset quiz.used.

There are just a few remaining concepts to handle. We need to code reset_record and reset_used, like this:

FunctionsCore/lib/mastery/core/quiz.ex
```
  defp reset_record(%{current_question: question} = quiz) do
    Map.put(
      quiz,
      :record,
      Map.delete(quiz.record, question.template.name)
    )
  end

  defp reset_used(%{current_question: question} = quiz) do
    Map.put(
      quiz,
      :used,
      List.delete(quiz.used, question.template)
    )
  end
end
```

Those functions are trivial. In each case, we update the quiz with a Map.put. reset_record deletes the record for a template, and reset_used deletes a question template from quiz.used. With that last detail, we're done. Let's take it for a spin!

Try Out the Core

IEx is a great tool to sanity check our code as we go. We're not going to run an exhaustive test; we'll save that work for the test chapter (Chapter 5, Test Your Core, on page 75). We'll use IEx to do a quick integration check to make sure our tools work together as we expect.

To do any meaningful integration test, we need a quiz but before we can build one we'll need a template. Our quiz will use a single template for addition that generates questions of the form "x + y". Type iex -S mix to open the codebase interactively:

```
$ iex -S mix
iex(1)> alias Mastery.Core.{Template, Quiz, Response}
[Mastery.Core.Template, Mastery.Core.Quiz, Mastery.Core.Response]
iex(2)> generator = %{ left: [1, 2], right: [1, 2] }
%{left: [1, 2], right: [1, 2]}
iex(3)> checker = fn(sub, answer) ->
...(3)>   sub[:left] + sub[:right] == String.to_integer(answer)
...(3)> end
#Function<12.99386804/2 in :erl_eval.expr/5>
```

We get the aliases out of the way before moving on to the generator and checker functions our template will need. The generator uses two short lists of integers and the checker tests that the answer is left + right. The user data will arrive in string form so we account for that with the String.to_integer/1 function.

Next we'll create a quiz, and then add the template with the pieces we've created, like this:

```
iex(4)> quiz = Quiz.new(title: "Addition", mastery: 2) \
...(4)> |> Quiz.add_template(
...(4)>       name: :single_digit_addition,
...(4)>       category: :addition,
...(4)>       instructions: "Add the numbers",
...(4)>       raw: "<%= @left %> + <%= @right %>",
...(4)>       generators: generator,
...(4)>       checker: checker ) \
...(4)> |> Quiz.select_question
%Mastery.Core.Quiz{
  current_question: %Mastery.Core.Question{
    asked: "1 + 2",
    substitutions: [left: 1, right: 2],
    template: %Mastery.Core.Template{
      category: :addition,
      checker: #Function<12.99386804/2 in :erl_eval.expr/5>,
      compiled: {...},
      generators: %{left: [1, 2], right: [1, 2]},
      instructions: "Add the numbers",
      name: :single_digit_addition,
      raw: "<%= @left %> + <%= @right %>"
    }
  },
  last_response: nil,
  mastered: [],
  mastery: 2,
  record: %{},
  templates: %{ addition: [...] },
  title: "Addition",
  used: []
}
```

Perfect. Our new quiz looks like it should with an empty record, nothing yet mastered and a single addition category for templates. Let's create an incorrect response, like this:

```
iex(5)> email="jill@example.com"
"jill@example.com"
iex(6)> response = Response.new(quiz, email, "0")
%Mastery.Core.Response{
  answer: "0",
  correct: false,
  email: "jill@example.com",
  quiz_title: "Addition",
  template_name: :single_digit_addition,
  timestamp: #DateTime<2019-03-31 20:59:12.823720Z>,
  to: "1 + 2"
}
iex(7)> quiz = Quiz.answer_question(quiz, response)
%Mastery.Core.Quiz{...}
iex(8)> quiz.record
%{}
```

We create a response. Mastery runs checkers as it creates the responses to make debugging and inspection easier so you can see that the response is incorrect. We advance our token with answer_question/2 and just as we expect, the record field remains empty.

Let's try a correct response instead:

```
iex(9)> quiz = Quiz.select_question(quiz)
%Mastery.Core.Quiz{...}
iex(10)> quiz.current_question.asked
"1 + 2"
iex(11)> response = Response.new quiz, email, "3"
%Mastery.Core.Response{
  answer: "3",
  correct: true,
  email: "jill@example.com",
  quiz_title: "Addition",
  template_name: :single_digit_addition,
  timestamp: #DateTime<2019-03-31 20:59:43.820340Z>,
  to: "1 + 2"
}
iex(12)> quiz = Quiz.answer_question(quiz, response)
%Mastery.Core.Quiz{...}
iex(13)> quiz.record
%{single_digit_addition: 1}
```

Perfect. We create a new question, check the question text and build a new correct response. Next, we advance our token with answer_question/2 and check the question record. Fortunately, we get a record of 1 for our :single_digit_addition template.

It works! We're tracking incorrect and correct answers correctly. We'll work through mastery in the next chapter. For now, we can take a deep breath and wrap up.

Build Your Functional Core

In this chapter, we showed how to build a functional core. It's mostly datatypes and code made up of strictly functions in modules, with the same inputs producing the same outputs as often as you can. The functional core has no processes and invokes no external services. It encapsulates the bulk of the business logic.

We also built the functional core of our Mastery project. Along the way, we embraced some core programming principles.

- Build single-purpose functions
- Where possible, bring functions to data rather than bringing your data to functions.
- Name concepts with functions
- Shape functions for composition
- Build functions at a single level of abstraction
- Make decisions in function heads where possible

We'll try to keep as much business logic and complexity as possible in the functional core. Building code this way makes it much easier to reason about functions, since the same inputs will always have the same outputs making testing much simpler.

In the next chapter, we'll exercise our functions in tests. We'll be getting some tests in while the system is easy to understand and tests are easy to shape, without any external interfaces or processes. When you're ready, turn the page!

CHAPTER 5

Test Your Core

If you're like us, you've been continuously asking a nagging question as we wrestled the data design and functional core to the ground. Where are the tests?

Here's a confession. We don't write code the way it's presented in this book. In real life, we make more mistakes, switch between data, functions, and tests often. We have debates, spike on feature branches, and we almost always create a test baseline as we go.

That coding style is a great way to work, but a lousy way to write a book like this, and with good reason. A book about layers can't jerk its readers breathlessly from layer to layer and still hope to teach the core concepts of each one. That's why we are going to present the tests, fully formed, line by line giving you the usual commentary of supporting theory and our thought process as we go.

We believe strongly that tests matter, test designs impact product designs, and testing as a whole has a tremendous impact on everything a development organization does. Rather than distributing bits of knowledge throughout the book, we decided to consolidate all of the testing philosophy and discussion to two different chapters, one for the core layers and one for the boundary layers.

Tests are the "T" for "things" in "Do fun things with big, loud worker-bees." You can see how they fit into the big picture as shown in the figure on page 76.

In this chapter, we'll lay out tests for the whole functional core. We will pay special attention to setup and composition. That strategy will allow us to build much more concise tests that tell a story. Later, our boundary tests will handle our boundary, lifecycle, and worker layers (in Chapter 10, Test the Boundary, on page 195).

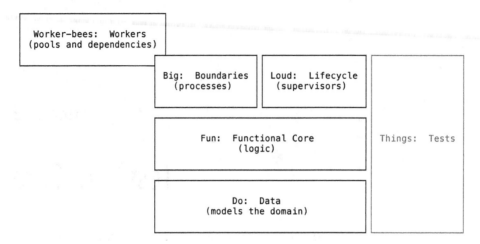

Do fun things with big, loud worker-bees.

If you're writing tests, you already know about ExUnit,[1] Elixir's sole framework for running unit tests. We're not going to tell you how it works because we want to spend time on *concepts* rather than *mechanics*. We'll suggest tools for coverage and property testing, but we won't show you those in practice. We believe in those concepts, but it would take a whole book to cover all of them. Instead, we'll mention the tools and techniques that will let you build your own testing philosophy.

When you're done, you'll be able to raise your thought process from individual tests to building systems of tests with supporting functions that compose. You'll be able to take a chaotic mix of code and refactor it so that the story beneath shines true. It all starts with a plan.

In broad strokes, this is our plan. We will focus as much effort as possible on composable functions for setup. Though we can test simple functions in isolation, the complex ones will require composition. We'll test the harder concepts with pipelines and custom test functions called fixtures.

A fixture is a bit of code in a test that sets up project code for convenient testing. In the core layer, fixtures return *data*. Investing in this setup code will take longer at first, but as our project grows in complexity our test cases will have the organizational structure to grow with the rest of our codebase.

Let's look at that plan in the context of ExUnit. Consider a typical test. Testing frameworks typically separate the tests into three broad pieces:

---

1.   https://elixirschool.com/en/lessons/basics/testing/

- Shared *setup* code prepares tests for execution. Their job is to lay a common foundation for experiments.

- A typical *test* compares expectations with actual results.

- Shared *teardown* code cleans up any side effects, so one test does not impact the rest.

Since we're testing our functional core (which is mostly pure), we won't need teardown code. All of our effort in this chapter will be on the setup and tests. As we go, we'll point out where to focus our attention. Let's put that plan into action.

Simplify Tests with Common Setup Functions

When we decided to write this book, one of our strongest desires was to solve a nontrivial problem. Recall that Mastery is the project we've been working on throughout this book. The project illustrates tests well because it has an intricate structure with many moving parts. Mastery quiz designers need to build complex structures. Mastery end users will answer questions with wrong and right answers, and the sequencing of questions will change based on those responses. Testing this flow is nontrivial, and here's why.

Writing tests is about establishing a flow. In each test, we prepare a question, ask the question, and compare the actual response with our expectations. As the domain grows in complexity, preparing for a question will take more and more effort.

In specific terms, for Mastery we must create quizzes with templates, as a teacher would, and then answer the questions those quizzes generate, as a user would. It's not just enough for our tests to answer questions in isolation. We must prove that users repeat sections until they achieve mastery by getting enough answers right. A substantial amount of this work is creating quizzes in the first place.

Here's the point. You must get setup right to get the rest of your tests right. Creating complex data structures to prepare for a test takes space on your editor page and space in your brain. Both are limited. Tests that pack too much into the test function itself obscure the purpose of the test so we'll put substantial effort into extracting common code from tests into setup.

We're going to use two primary types of setup. One type, called *fixtures*, are functions that return data structures. We can call fixtures from anywhere in our tests. The second kind of setup code, called *named setups*, are functions that create project-specific data and place it into data structures that we'll pass directly into our tests as formal parameters. Let's look at each one in greater detail.

Fixtures are constructors. They are convenience functions that return complex, project-specific structures for the purposes of tests. We'll build fixtures to create quizzes, templates, and the other kinds of data structures we'll need to put Mastery through its paces. A convenient place to put such data is the test *context*.

Whether you need it or not, ExUnit has a special argument, called a context, to track metadata about each individual test. The context is a Map that has all of the data Elixir needs to run a test, such as the name of the test case and so on. Conveniently, developers can add test-specific data to the context as well. Since contexts are maps, they are easy to work with.

Rather than giving each test the responsibility of creating all of its own test data, we will use *named setup* functions to build a common set of data that works across several tests and load it into the context. Named setups are essentially test fixtures. Like other fixtures for the core layer, they return data. Named setups are special because:

- They are functions with a specific signature. They take a context and return an {:ok, context} tuple.

- They return test data that they put into the context.

Tests can then invoke named setups by name to set up specific scenarios. We'll go into them in detail in the sections that follow, but first we will look at a trick for making our tests less noisy by stripping away unnecessary ceremony. To do so, we'll need to make a brief detour into the ExUnit test helpers.

Improve the ExUnit Infrastructure

Improving our setup is important, but it's not enough. We can also improve our tests by stripping away ceremony and organizing our infrastructure. Things like common aliases and helper functions can quickly cut a couple of dozen characters in half. In a nutshell, these tiny bits of infrastructure will make it easier for our users to invoke the setups that improve our tests.

Normally, we'd add a few aliases to the top of a file and call it a day, but we'll often have several different test files that need to use the same lines. Instead of tacking the same aliases to multiple files, we need a way to reuse these lines. Let's pay a visit to the man behind the curtain to see how we'll do that work.

When mix new project_name creates a new project, it builds a test directory with two files. One is a simple test with a single line of consequence: use ExUnit.Case. That statement is a macro that includes all the macros and functions our tests will need. One of the things that macro does is include the file test/test_helper.exs. Let's open it up and see what's inside:

```
ExUnit.start()
```

This helper starts the ExUnit process that will run our tests. It's an ideal place to put the additional ceremony our project will need, things like aliases or imports for our project modules or setup functions. We'll use test/test_helper.exs to import the testing fixtures our project will need, like this:

Tests/test/test_helper.exs
```
Code.require_file "support/quiz_builders.exs", __DIR__

ExUnit.start()
```

We require support/quiz_builders.exs, which will have our fixtures that build quizzes, templates, and the like. Let's begin to build out our fixtures, and all of the machinery they will need to conveniently create quizzes. Crack that file open and let's get it started by adding a _using_ macro, like this:

Tests/test/support/quiz_builders.exs
```
defmodule QuizBuilders do
  defmacro __using__(_options) do
    quote do
      alias Mastery.Core.{Template, Response, Quiz}
      import QuizBuilders, only: :functions
    end
  end

  alias Mastery.Core.{Template, Question, Quiz}
```

We could easily just make this file a standalone module. That's not good enough for our tests. We want to remove the obstacle of processing the full module name, a test support name that's meaningless to our user, each of the hundreds of times we need to create test data. That means using a macro.

This one does two simple things. First, it aliases key modules so the user can use the abbreviated names. Then, it inserts the functions into the test module *as if those functions had been defined there*. Now, our quizzes can do

```
assert Quiz.function(build_data())
```

instead of

```
assert Mastery.Core.Quiz.function(Mastery.QuizBuilder.build_data())
```

Don't worry about the build_data function right now. It's just a placeholder as we work out the details.

Saving that bit of ceremony with the fully qualified Mastery.QuizBuilder is important since the test setup is such a big part of our overall testing experience. Alternatively, the test user could explicitly add an alias to the top of the test file to save that ceremony, but that strategy comes with its own limitations because you'd need to add the aliases to each test file. Either way, it's a substantial win.

With the machinery out of the way, let's add the constructors to QuizBuilders that will smooth out our tests.

Provide Test Data with Fixtures

We'll focus on fixtures in this section. Recall that in our functional core, test fixtures are functions that create data so we can write repeatable tests without the extra ceremony. Our quizzes are complex, so the job of our fixtures is to focus on building data—the various structs and maps that make up our data layer—so we can keep those details out of the tests.

Recall that our quizzes have the following structure:

```
defstruct title: nil,
          mastery: 3,
          templates: %{ },
          used: [ ],
          current_question: nil,
          record: %{ },
          last_response: nil,
          mastered: [ ]
```

We'll need to set those first three fields. The rest are computed. The best way to populate the templates field is to call our add_template function with a set of template fields.

That means our strategy is going to look something like this:

```
build_quiz
|> add_template(template_fields_1)
|> add_template(template_fields_2)
```

Templates are also complex, so we'll start with those. While you've got support/quiz_builders.exs open, add this code:

Tests/test/support/quiz_builders.exs
```
def template_fields(overrides \\ [ ]) do
  Keyword.merge(
    [
      name: :single_digit_addition,
      category: :addition,
      instructions: "Add the numbers",
      raw: "<%= @left %> + <%= @right %>",
      generators: addition_generators(single_digits()),
      checker: &addition_checker/2
    ],
    overrides
  )
end
```

That code looks nasty, but most of the job is delegated to other functions. The rest sets up the raw fields our templates will need. Those fields set up a template for single-digit addition. We have functions to set up the generators and checkers we need. We wrap those fields in a Keyword.merge so the user can customize our default templates with fields of their own.

Now we can look ahead to the functions that support these fields. Add the following to support/quiz_builders.exs, like this:

Tests/test/support/quiz_builders.exs
```
def double_digit_addition_template_fields() do
  template_fields(
    name: :double_digit_addition,
    generators: addition_generators(double_digits())
  )
end

def addition_generators(left, right \\ nil) do
  %{left: left, right: right || left}
end

def double_digits() do
  Enum.to_list(10..99)
end

def single_digits() do
  Enum.to_list(0..9)
end
```

We have a function that provides template fields for double-digit addition. It uses a helper function to build out the generators. A generator is a map where the keys are fields and the values are substitutions for those fields.

Next we have three trivial helper functions to help build generators. The first builds a generator map we'll use for all addition templates. It has :left and :right substitutions. If the user provides only one list, the function will use the same list for both :left and :right. The next two functions provide single-digit and double-digit lists for addition substitutions.

The last piece of templates is the checkers. Add them to support/quiz_builders now:

```
Tests/test/support/quiz_builders.exs
def addition_checker(substitutions, answer) do
  left = Keyword.fetch!(substitutions, :left)
  right = Keyword.fetch!(substitutions, :right)
  to_string(left + right) == String.trim(answer)
end
```

They fetch :left and :right from the template and then add them together, and compare the result to a string. We use Keyword.fetch! because we want to know immediately if the field is missing, and it will raise an error rather than returning a nil value.

Now with the templates out of the way, the heavy lifting is mostly done. We can focus on building quizzes. That's nearly trivial now:

```
Tests/test/support/quiz_builders.exs
def quiz_fields(overrides) do
  Keyword.merge([title: "Simple Arithmetic"], overrides)
end

def build_quiz(quiz_overrides \\ []) do
  quiz_overrides
  |> quiz_fields
  |> Quiz.new
end

def build_question(overrides \\ [ ]) do
  overrides
  |> template_fields
  |> Template.new
  |> Question.new
end
```

Our quiz_fields function returns some default attributes and merges in overrides. Then all build_quiz has to do is take the overrides, pipe them into quiz_fields, and pipe that into Quiz.new. Lovely.

Building a question is also easy. Since we need only a template to generate a question, we have all we need. We take our overrides, pipe them into template_fields, pipe that into Template.new and pipe that into Question.new. Our work to keep our functions composable is paying off.

It's time to see the benefits of all of our hard work. We're going to build a quiz with two templates. That code looks like this:

```
Tests/test/support/quiz_builders.exs
  def build_quiz_with_two_templates(quiz_overrides \\ []) do
    build_quiz(quiz_overrides)
    |> Quiz.add_template(template_fields())
    |> Quiz.add_template(double_digit_addition_template_fields())
  end
end
```

That uses the composition tools we've already built to construct a template. Let's try our shiny new QuizBuilders module.

Use Fixture Functions Directly

We have a single test we'll need for templates. We want to make sure templates get compiled correctly. That test would be difficult if we had to do all of the setup work in the test block itself. Instead, we'll use the helper functions in QuizBuilders to bang our test out quickly.

Open up test/template_test.exs and add your new test, like this:

```
Tests/test/template_test.exs
defmodule TemplateTest do
  use ExUnit.Case
  use QuizBuilders

  test "building compiles the raw template" do
    fields = template_fields()
    template = Template.new(fields)

    assert is_nil(Keyword.get(fields, :compiled))
    assert not is_nil(template.compiled)
  end
end
```

The test is pretty tight. We get our default template fields for single-digit addition. Then we use those to build a template. Finally, we check to make sure the compiled keyword is nil in fields, but set in the template. The purpose of our test shines through and we can be confident in our new tools.

Simplify Tests with Custom Data Fixtures

Here's what we've done so far. Our testers can now build a large quiz in parts. They can provide overrides for the overall quiz. If they need to build something more custom, they can use the composable tools to generate template fields and add those in whatever combinations they choose. So our data layer has three main properties, and all are important:

- It allows one-shot creation of complex concepts, our quiz.

- It supports composition of complex options by exposing the constructors for the simple ones.

- It exposes overrides to all core functions so that individual fields can be changed.

In short, we moved the tedious repeated setup features out of the line of sight of a typical test and into a custom toolbox that *all* tests can use. Now let's put those tools to work.

Prime Tests with Named Setups

You've just seen the first type of setup function, fixtures. In this section, we'll cover the next kind of reusable setup function, ExUnit's *named setup* feature. To understand how it works, let's take a more detailed look at the flow of a typical ExUnit testcase.

In version 1.3 of Elixir, the ExUnit.Case module added a *describe block*. Tests within a block could share common setup code. When you specified a block of tests within a describe, you could also specify the names of one or more functions to create common setup data. Here's how that would look, in our test layer:

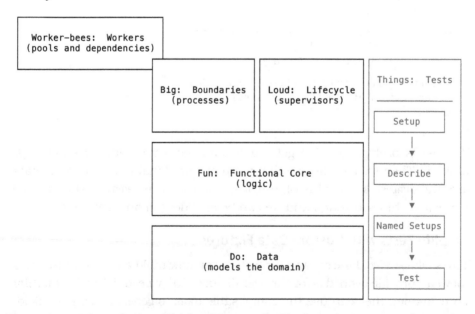

You can see how tests with describe work. Each test runs common setup code, then a describe block, then any named setups specified by that describe block, and then the test itself. Each one of those functions takes a common context, a simple map that has all of the metadata required to run a test.

Describe blocks add a little bit of ceremony to the ExUnit flow, but this extra little bit of complexity in the framework can go a long way toward simplifying individual tests by moving common setup code into one or more named setups.

A *named setup* is a function that does one thing. It takes an ExUnit context and adds project-specific data to it. Here's what a named setup function looks like:

```
def setup_function(context) do
  {:ok, Map.put(context, :test_data, build_your_test_data() )}
end
```

It takes a context and returns a success tuple with a revised context. Every named setup will have this same shape.

Now, if many functions need access to the same value in :test_data, you can block those tests into a describe, like this:

```
describe "a group of tests needing :test_data" do
  setup [:setup_function]

  test "a test", %{test_data: data} do
    assert MyModule.my_function(data) == :ok
  end

  test "another test", %{test_data: data} do
    assert MyModule.another_function(data) == :ok
  end
end
```

Keep in mind that the context is just a map. It's the common data structure that ties ExUnit together, just as Quiz ties Mastery together. It contains the private and custom data each test needs.

You might have noticed that the setup function takes a list rather than an atom. That means you can pass multiple named setup functions, like this:

```
describe "a group of tests needing :test_data" do
  setup [:setup_function, :another_setup_function]
```

Since all named setups have the same signature and they all compose over the same token, you can have as many setups as you want. It's a wonderful way to name the preconditions your tests need to run.

We now have some fixtures we've established in our QuizBuilders module and know about the named setup feature, so we can apply those tools to our tests.

All of this setup code may seem like too much boiler plate for such a small test suite. Keep in mind that our test suite is not complete. We're building enough tests to make sure we're giving you a book with code that works—a full production test suite would usually be much larger. The investments we've made will increasingly pay off as the test suite grows. Each new test multiplies these benefits:

- You have less duplication
- The purpose for each test becomes more clear across teams
- Your codebase will grow much more slowly

With the trade-offs in mind, we're going to choose to write some named setups to control duplication and to simplify each test block. Let's start with test/response_test.exs since it's complex enough to need named setups but simple enough to illustrate the concept. The first step is to create the file with the basic heading, like this:

Tests/test/response_test.exs
```
defmodule ResponseTest do
  use ExUnit.Case
  use QuizBuilders
```

We use the QuizBuilders macro to build in our fixtures. Next, we'll build a simple local function to build a quiz with the exact quiz and templates we need, like this:

Tests/test/response_test.exs
```
defp quiz() do
  fields = template_fields(generators: %{left: [1], right: [2]})

  build_quiz()
  |> Quiz.add_template(fields)
  |> Quiz.select_question
end

defp response(answer) do
  Response.new(quiz(), "mathy@example.com", answer)
end
```

Since we're testing for correct responses, we want a repeatable template with only one possible correct answer, "3". That means we'll build a custom addition template with single item lists containing [1] and [2]. When our generator fires, it will create a question with the problem 1 + 2.

We also create a response using the answer provided by the user, our custom quiz function and a hardcoded email address.

Now we can use those functions to create trivial named setups, like this:

Tests/test/response_test.exs
```
  defp right(context) do
    { :ok, Map.put(context, :right, response("3")) }
  end

  defp wrong(context) do
    { :ok, Map.put(context, :wrong, response("2")) }
  end
end
```

We have a right setup and a wrong one. The names right and wrong are important, both as function names and keys in the context map. They clearly indicate the types of responses in the context.

All that remains is the need to use those keys in the context. Add this code after the use macros:

Tests/test/response_test.exs
```
describe "a right response and a wrong response" do
  setup [:right, :wrong]

  test "building responses checks answers", %{right: right, wrong: wrong} do
    assert right.correct
    refute wrong.correct
  end

  test "a timestamp is added at build time", %{right: response} do
    assert %DateTime{ } = response.timestamp
    assert response.timestamp < DateTime.utc_now()
  end
end
```

The describe serves two purposes. It puts tests in a named group and also provides the scope for the named setups. The group of tests will have a right and a wrong response in the context. Not every test will use every value in the context, and that's OK. Presumably as we add tests to this script to make our suite more robust, we'll be able to leverage these same setup details for at least some of them.

Next, let's explore the tests themselves, even though there's not much to say. The line assert right.correct is beautifully descriptive—we expect right answers to be correct. We pattern match to get the assignments out of the body of the test block and into the function head. We can assert different things about each response: that we're correctly firing the checker functions, that we're creating appropriate timestamps, and the like.

Notice how clear the purpose of each test becomes. Building a response is complicated. It requires a question, which requires a template, which requires generators, checkers, and a quiz. We hide the complexity from the user and let them slowly dig into the details, one layer of abstraction at a time.

Also notice that we needed a completely custom quiz with predictable answers. That quiz was easy to build because we got the abstraction right. We build a base quiz and pipe that through add_template with our overrides to give us exactly what we need.

Finally notice that changes to new Response structs are limited to a few lines of code in our codebase. This abstraction feels right so far. We still need to see how our setup functions deal with both very simple tests and more complicated ones in the tests to come.

With our QuizBuilders working, we can shift our attention to other tests. Let's deal with a sticky problem, dealing with functions that are not pure.

Make Tests Repeatable

All of our tests are inside our functional core. In the core, calling a function with the same arguments will *almost* always result in the same output. That word "almost" is a killer because our whole strategy involves comparing our expectations to actual values. When we can't have expectations from run to run, we must change our approach.

Sometimes, functions are not perfectly pure. Functions that create timestamps or random numbers are famously difficult to test. We have both types of functions in our codebase. For example, recall the response test:

```
test "a timestamp is added at build time", %{right: response} do
  assert %DateTime{ } = response.timestamp
  assert response.timestamp < DateTime.utc_now
end
```

We deal with that problem by changing the way we think about expectations. Rather than testing against an explicit value, we make sure the timestamp is in fact a timestamp, and that it's before the present moment, utc_now.

Random numbers will be a little trickier. As we build out the tests in our test/question_test.exs file, we'll dodge the random problem in most of them by building tests that restrict choices in one way or another. Let's solve the easy problems first and save the toughest for last.

First, we need the typical test directives:

Tests/test/question_test.exs
```
defmodule QuestionTest do
  use ExUnit.Case
  use QuizBuilders
```

Next, we'll ensure generators make a choice from a list. Rather than deal with random numbers right off the bat, we'll restrict the template to two lists of one, like this:

Tests/test/question_test.exs
```
test "building chooses substitutions" do
  question = build_question(generators: addition_generators([1], [2]))

  assert question.substitutions == [left: 1, right: 2]
end
```

We generate a template for single-digit addition with two lists of a single item. Then we test against the expected substitutions.

Here's a trivial approach to dealing with our random number nemesis. Lists of one certainly simplify the test because we know exactly what the result should be. In this case, we can tell whether the choices get plugged into the substitutions correctly. We essentially stacked the deck.

We'll deal with a more complete test for the specific random problem in a bit. For now, let's make sure other types of generators work, like this:

Tests/test/question_test.exs
```
test "function generators are called" do
  generators = addition_generators( fn -> 42 end, [0] )
  substitutions = build_question(generators: generators).substitutions

  assert Keyword.fetch!(substitutions, :left) == generators.left.()
end
```

That's an interesting test. We pass in a function as one of the generators for a custom template. We'll include a function that returns 42, the most important number in the universe.[2] Then, we fire the generator, and compare the value of the substitution to the value the function returns. Once again, we stack the deck in our favor by picking a very simple function to use in our generator.

The test is simple because we already know Elixir can reliably compute custom functions, so we don't need to test that. We need only test that our generator fires a function, so a simple one works fine.

---

2. https://www.urbandictionary.com/define.php?term=42

With function and list generators in our pocket, we can move on to computing the asked field for questions. Once again, we don't really care how the values are chosen. We only care that the correct values get plugged in. We'll use a simple template once again, like this:

Tests/test/question_test.exs
```
test "building creates asked question text" do
  question = build_question(generators: addition_generators([1], [2]))

  assert question.asked == "1 + 2"
end
```

Once again, we provide two lists of one item, making the generated text easy to compare. The test becomes trivial.

We've successfully dodged the idea of random numbers, but it's time to pay the piper. We have to pay for the fact that we don't have repeatable results when we generate a question using random numbers, so we'll have to improvise.

We can use streams to generate many random numbers, and then narrow that value to the one we need, like this:

Tests/test/question_test.exs
```
  test "a random choice is made from list generators" do
    generators = addition_generators(Enum.to_list(1..9), [0])

    assert eventually_match(generators, 1)
    assert eventually_match(generators, 9)
  end

  def eventually_match(generators, answer) do
    Stream.repeatedly(fn ->
      build_question(generators: generators).substitutions
    end)
    |> Enum.find(fn substitution ->
      Keyword.fetch!(substitution, :left) == answer end)
    end
  end
end
```

This time, our generator picks a random number from a list from 1 to 9. That means we need to get creative. We don't want to test that Elixir creates a specific number, because that defeats the nature of the tool we built. We want to test that Elixir eventually picks a number we expect. We'll choose to pick the edges of our random function, the digits 1 and 9.

Here's the magic. We start from the same foundation, the generators created at the top of the test. Building on the same foundation is important, and what makes this test a strong one. We want to make sure that this exact generator will eventually generate a specific number we're calling answer. We use Stream.repeatedly to let our generator build an endless stream of substitutions, and we then convert the stream to an enumerable with Enum.find. That means we'll get random numbers until we hit the one we're looking for. Keep in mind that this approach is not the only one that we could have chosen:

- We could have reseeded our random number generator so that our random function generated a predictable list.

- We could've made our random function pluggable and picked a deterministic function for our tests and a random one for our other environments.

- We could've checked ranges.

The point is not which solution we chose but that we made a trade-off. We chose to complicate our tests to build the impure random function into our functional core and had to deal with some extra complexity in our tests as a result. We think the trade-off is a good one, but you can choose to make a different one.

With this tricky random-number problem out of the way, it's time to look to the next significant challenge. Let's take on the six-headed hydra, the beast we call Quiz.

Compose Within Tests

The most complex module is Quiz because that's the module that holds state as we progress through a test. It needs to generate questions from templates, cycle through templates, track mastery, and finish when mastery is complete. We've put it off as long as we can. We need to slay this beast. We'll attack it with our setups and by composing through our token, the Quiz.

Crack open test/quiz_test.exs to construct our quiz. Start with the typical ceremony, the module plus the two use directives, like this:

Tests/test/quiz_test.exs
```
defmodule QuizTest do
  use ExUnit.Case
  use QuizBuilders
```

Next, we'll need helper functions, one that handles random question generation and one to build a convenient shortcut to return the template for a quiz, like this:

```
Tests/test/quiz_test.exs
defp eventually_pick_other_template(quiz, template) do
  Stream.repeatedly(fn ->
    Quiz.select_question(quiz).current_question.template
  end)
  |> Enum.find(fn other -> other != template end)
end

defp template(quiz) do
  quiz.current_question.template
end
```

After we build a question, we know the generators will eventually build another one. Just as we did in our Question test, we Stream.repeatedly, creating questions until we eventually find a question that is different from the one that's passed in.

The next function, template, is just to save typing because we're lazy. Let's make a few more helpers, this time to answer questions like this:

```
Tests/test/quiz_test.exs
defp right_answer(quiz), do: answer_question(quiz, "3")
defp wrong_answer(quiz), do: answer_question(quiz, "wrong")

defp answer_question(quiz, answer) do
  email = "mathy@example.com"
  response = Response.new(quiz, email, answer)
  Quiz.answer_question(quiz, response)
end
```

The first two functions generate right and wrong answers using a third function. It just passes data straight through to the quiz. Notice that these functions all take and return a Quiz. This trick will help us compose complex flows.

Now, we'll add a few more functions to serve as named setups, like this:

```
Tests/test/quiz_test.exs
defp quiz(context) do
  {:ok, Map.put(context, :quiz, build_quiz_with_two_templates())}
end

defp quiz_always_adds_one_and_two(context) do
  fields = template_fields(generators: addition_generators([1], [2]))

  quiz =
    build_quiz(mastery: 2)
    |> Quiz.add_template(fields)

  {:ok, Map.put(context, :quiz, quiz)}
end
```

They build quizzes using the functions we created in QuizBuilders, and return the :ok tuple. The first builds the default quiz with two templates. We'll use that one to make sure our quiz cycles through templates as it should. The second builds a template with predictable answers. We'll use that one to test mastery.

We need one more piece before we write our tests. We'd like to compose our tests with long, simple pipelines that tell a story, but we want to do some assertions in the midst of the pipeline. We build a couple of helper functions that just change the shape of assertions, like this:

Tests/test/quiz_test.exs
```
  defp assert_more_questions(quiz) do
    refute is_nil(quiz)
    quiz
  end

  defp refute_more_questions(quiz) do
    assert is_nil(quiz)
    quiz
  end
end
```

These functions are dead simple, but they will have a tremendous impact on our tests. They take a quiz and return one, but do an assertion in the middle. An assertion is effectively a side effect. This technique will let us put together a longer flow when we want to test a mastery.

It's finally time to write some tests. Add these tests at the top of the file, after the use directives. First, we need to make sure we're generating random questions. Here's the approach:

Tests/test/quiz_test.exs
```
describe "when a quiz has two templates" do
  setup [:quiz]

  test "the next question is randomly selected", %{quiz: quiz} do
    %{current_question: %{template: first_template}} =
      Quiz.select_question(quiz)

    other_template = eventually_pick_other_template(quiz, first_template)
    assert first_template != other_template
  end
```

This is the first of two tests that use named setups to hide the complexity of data creation by creating our quiz outside of the test block. Our tests are primed with the correct templates, and we have a function that will take the same template and keep generating questions *with that same template* until it eventually finds a question that doesn't match the first one. It's the same technique we used when testing random substitution generation.

Next, we have a test that makes sure we cycle through all templates until we've exhausted them. Remember, it's still in the describe block with the same named setup that calls quiz:

Tests/test/quiz_test.exs
```
  test "templates are unique until cycle repeats", %{quiz: quiz} do
    first_quiz  = Quiz.select_question(quiz)
    second_quiz = Quiz.select_question(first_quiz)
    reset_quiz  = Quiz.select_question(second_quiz)

    assert template(first_quiz) != template(second_quiz)
    assert template(reset_quiz) in [template(first_quiz), template(second_quiz)]
  end
end
```

This test is tricky because once again we have random generation. We expect our quiz to generate two questions and then reset, but we don't know in which order. We generate the first and second questions, and make sure the first two templates for those questions are different. Then, we make sure that the third question's template, the one we expect to be reset, is from the list of the first two. It may take you a while to follow the logic, but it's correct.

Finally, we need to test mastery. Since we have one template with a mastery of two, and since a wrong question resets mastery, we need to generate a test that goes something like quiz |> right |> wrong |> right |> right, and that should finish the quiz. We can generate a test that's almost as clear, like this:

Tests/test/quiz_test.exs
```
describe "a quiz that always adds one and two" do
  setup [:quiz_always_adds_one_and_two]

  test "a wrong answer resets mastery", %{quiz: quiz} do
    quiz
    |> Quiz.select_question
    |> assert_more_questions
    |> right_answer
    |> Quiz.select_question
    |> assert_more_questions
    |> wrong_answer
    |> Quiz.select_question
    |> assert_more_questions
    |> right_answer
    |> Quiz.select_question
    |> assert_more_questions
    |> right_answer
    |> Quiz.select_question
    |> refute_more_questions
  end
end
```

These kinds of tests can get difficult to read without composition, but with it, the story we're trying to tell comes through beautifully.

We have taken this test as far as we should in this single chapter, but there are still a couple more details to cover.

Take Tests Beyond the Elixir Base

Testing is a broad topic and a controversial one. The Elixir community has so far shown pretty basic tastes as far as testing tools go. In this section, we'll look at a couple of interesting places where Elixir programmers are using more cutting-edge techniques for testing a functional core.

The first idea, code coverage, is that you should understand what's tested and what's not. Elixir has built-in tools to help you do so.

The second is that you can use tools to let your system generate many different test inputs automatically and test those inputs against known properties of your code. The technique, called property-based testing, has been around for a while but is picking up momentum in the Elixir community.

Consider Measuring the Reach of Your Tests

Many teams think it's important to know the reach of their tests. The mix tool allows coverage tracking. We suggest that you have a coverage threshold as a metric for your project. If the coverage falls below the metric, you can react accordingly.

We don't need to do anything to check coverage for the code we've built so far. Run mix test --cover in a console that's in the root directory of mastery, like this:

```
~/mastery → mix test --cover
...
Cover compiling modules ...
...

Percentage | Module
-----------|--------------------------
   100.00% | Mastery.Core.Quiz
   100.00% | Mastery.Application
   100.00% | Mastery.Core.Template
   100.00% | Mastery
    87.50% | Mastery.Core.Response
    87.50% | Mastery.Core.Question
-----------|--------------------------
    77.50% | Total

Generated HTML coverage results in 'cover' directory
```

Notice that two of the lines are showing uncovered. Those lines have defstruct macros on them, and they are not showing that they are covered, though we clearly defined those structs and exercised them in our functions. If you are looking for a threshold below 100%, that's OK. If you're trying to maintain full coverage, you'll often need a tool with a little more configurability.

The ExCoveralls tool[3] can work as a replacement for the default coverage provided by ExUnit. All you need to do is add the hex dependency, and add this line to your mix.exs:

```
test_coverage: [tool: ExCoveralls]
```

Then you can run it with mix coveralls. See the documentation for more details. One of the nice things about ExCoveralls is that you can build a configuration file to control what's counted and what's ignored. As always, use the tool that works best for you.

Now that you know how to find out whether all of your lines are covered, we can look at another advanced testing technique. Property-based tests show how to automate your test creation.

Consider Property-Based Tests

In these examples, we've focused on unit testing. These kinds of tests pass predetermined values to our functional core and measure the impact with assertions. Another testing strategy is *property-based testing*. Fred Hebert has an excellent book on property-based testing, *Property-Based Testing with PropEr, Erlang, and Elixir [Heb19]*. The *PropEr* framework is an Erlang framework with good support for Elixir too.

In property-based testing, you'll define assumptions about the inputs called properties and outputs of a function and *let the computer generate values* to run through your tests. If the property holds true for all values, the test passes. If it does not, the test fails, and simplifies the set of inputs that break the assumptions. Here's an example from Fred's book:

```
property "a sorted list keeps its size" do
  forall l <- list(number()) do
    length(l) == length(Enum.sort(l))
  end
end
```

That test is much more powerful than the tests you see written in this chapter. list(number()) is a generator that creates a random list of numbers. For each

---

3.   https://github.com/parroty/excoveralls/blob/master/README.md

list, we make sure the length of the sorted list is the same as the length of the inbound list.

For token-based solutions like ours, these tests are especially powerful. We can generate a much more diverse set of inputs and outputs to run against our program. The topic is beyond the scope of this book. To learn more, see *Property-Based Testing with PropEr, Erlang, and Elixir [Heb19]* by Fred Hebert.

Test Your Functional Core

In this chapter, we've been busy. We've tested our functional core from end to end. Here's how we did it.

We started with setup functions to build our test data. Since our quiz is a complex model with many complex transitions, we needed some functions to let us quickly set up quizzes to simulate a variety of conditions. We used simple functions, and paid careful attention to composition. We also gave our functions the ability to override defaults.

Once we had those functions, we used them in named setups. Those functions are small composable purpose-built testing functions that layer complexity for tests. We tested templates, questions, and responses in this way.

Once we moved to the QuizTest, we needed more help. We leaned on the composable design of the quiz and the data helpers we built to write tests that told a story. We made sure our tests communicated our intent from the beginning.

Finally, we looked at some additional topics. We looked at the value of code coverage and property-based tests. We pointed out a few projects that are useful in that context.

This chapter concludes Part I. In Part II, we're going to look into how to use our functional cores to preserve state reliably but simply. Let's get busy!

Part II

...with Big, Loud Worker-Bees

Part II addresses the layers we'll implement with Elixir's OTP. We'll deal with the second part of the sentence "Do fun things with big, loud worker-bees." When you hear "big, loud worker-bees" think "boundaries, lifecycles, and workers."

These are the boundary layers. As a whole, they represent the process machinery that establishes processes (boundary), starts or stops them (lifecycle) and divides work (workers).

CHAPTER 6

Isolate Process Machinery in a Boundary

Boundaries are the "B" for "big" in the sentence "Do fun things with big, loud worker-bees." In Part I of this book, we handled the first half of that sentence. We built and tested the functional core that serves to isolate as much code as possible from processes. Remember, many projects will not need any layers beyond these three.

Part II deals with "big, loud worker-bees," the outer layers. These layers include all of the process machinery, message passing, and recursion that form the heart of concurrency in Elixir systems. The *boundary* cleanly executes core code in a process and wraps it in a generic API. The *lifecycle* layer provides tools to start and stop the boundary layer, even in the context of a larger project. *Workers* divide work for performance, isolation, or reliability. You'll see all of these layers in the following figure:

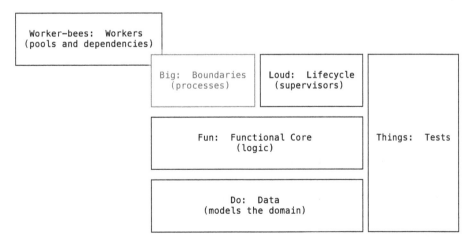

Do fun things with big, loud worker-bees.

In this chapter, we focus on the boundary, the process that wraps the business logic defined in the core. Our boundaries might share common state with other processes, communicate with remote servers, or isolate a critical service from failures in the rest of the system.

We will use OTP to implement our outer layers because it bakes in many of the concepts we'll need: a common API for dealing with initialization and messages we'll need in our boundary layer, the supervisors we'll need to build the lifecycle layer, and patterns we'll use to spin up workers.

Boundaries introduce additional complexity and uncertainty. The inputs and outputs of functions in the core are often trusted and well defined, but the boundary machinery must deal with uncertainty because our boundary API must process unsanitized user input and the external systems our boundary might use can fail. Let's look at some of the techniques our boundary can use to deal with uncertainty.

Maintain Composition Through Uncertainty

External services such as databases or network requests can unexpectedly slow down or fail; well-meaning users can make mistakes; malicious users can try to cause mischief with inputs shaped to attack our systems.

Though Elixir programmers depend on pipes, dealing with errors midstream in piped compositions is awkward and unreliable. As we build our boundary, we will need strategies for maintaining a composable architecture through this uncertainty.

Because our services may struggle under load, we may need to use *back pressure*, a technique to slow requests to those services under duress. Since the data will come from untrusted sources we must consider validations as we wrap our functional core in an API.

You may have noticed that we make heavy use of Elixir's |> operator. Often pipes rely on functions we expect to succeed. Since the boundary can't rely on this kind of certainty, we need to adopt new techniques.

Before we get back into the Mastery project we're building to take complex quizzes, let's address some of the techniques you might use to smooth out our boundary in spite of all that uncertainty. We'll work with errors as data, and dig into the with function, which will let us compose with functions that might fail.

Treat Errors as Data

Functional programs are simpler when we can use pipelines to simplify code. Transforming data is one of the fundamental tenets of Elixir, but there's a problem. Functions that fail often raise exceptions. When we don't handle errors, they transition to *code execution* in the form of exceptions.

Exceptions don't compose neatly and the resulting error codes aren't always informative. In this section, we'll examine ways to transform exceptions to data.

There's another problem with relying on pipes that fail midstream. You can often lose context. If you can treat errors as data, managing flows in pipelines gets a little bit simpler. With error data structures, later functions in a pipeline can decide how to handle them. You can report partial success, or even halt on an error with context, just as the Plug framework from Phoenix does.

Here's how it works. Let's define a worker with some artificial failure:

```
defmodule Worker do
  def work(n) do
    if :rand.uniform(10) == 1 do
      raise "Oops!"
    else
      {:result, :rand.uniform(n * 100)}
    end
  end
end
```

We write an intentionally buggy worker. A failure means an exception. We can turn that exception into data, like this:

```
def make_work_safe(dangerous_work, arg) do
  try do
    apply(dangerous_work, [arg])
  rescue
    error ->
      {:error, error, arg}  # include any needed context here
  end
end
```

It's a simple rescue. Now we can stream the work, like this:

```
  def stream_work do
    Stream.iterate(1, &(&1 + 1))
    |> Stream.map(fn i -> make_work_safe(&work/1, i) end)
  end
end
```

That function will iterate on our work forever. We map over the stream making the work function safe.

Now, let's put it to use, using the techniques we mentioned. First, let's report partial success as we go, until there's an error, like this:

```
IO.puts "Report partial success:"
Worker.stream_work
|> Enum.take(10)
|> IO.inspect
```

We can now report on a block of work, with some successes and some errors. Alternatively, we can report successes until we get to a failure, like this:

```
IO.puts "Halt on error with context:"
Worker.stream_work
|> Enum.reduce_while([ ], fn
  {:error, _error, _context} = error, _results ->
    {:halt, error}
  result, results ->
    {:cont, [result | results]}
end)
|> case do
     {:error, _error, _context} = error ->
       error
     results ->
       Enum.reverse(results)
   end
|> IO.inspect
```

In the first pipe block, we reduce over the code using Enum.reduce_while. This function will reduce until the function returns a {:halt, error} tuple. If there's an error, we return an error tuple. Otherwise, we collect the results.

In the second pipe block, we either return an error or reverse the results.

Running this code will give you something like this:

```
$ elixir pipeline_errors.exs
Report partial success:
[
 {:result, 58},
 {:result, 127},
 {:error, %RuntimeError{message: "Oops!"}, 3},
 {:result, 275},
 {:result, 488},
 {:error, %RuntimeError{message: "Oops!"}, 6},
 {:result, 511},
 {:result, 608},
 {:result, 238},
 {:result, 751}
]
Halt on error with context:
{:error, %RuntimeError{message: "Oops!"}, 5}
```

Mastery works with two versions of this problem. The first is collecting all of the validation errors related to a single piece of input. The second is composing over functions that might fail with validation errors. We've talked about the first, translating errors to data. Let's address the second, composing over functions that might fail.

Use with to Compose Uncertain Structures

The philosophy of with is simple. It allows you to specify pattern matches at each step of composition. If the match succeeds, the composition proceeds. If it fails, the composition halts and falls through to an else condition.

Here's an example from later in this chapter. We will build an API layer that has to validate data. The functions will have to have ugly if-then logic rather than simple compositions. We'll use with to smooth out the rough edges.

Here's how the approach works. First, let's say we're building a new quiz with data provided by the user. We'd like to pass validated data to a service that stores quizzes like this:

```
def new(quiz_fields) do
  quiz_fields
  |> validate_quiz
  |> QuizManager.build_quiz
end
```

The problem is that the output of validate_quiz will have a different shape, and will need different logic to support the data. Also, our validation API doesn't compose the way we want it to. If validation fails, we want to deal with the error, like this:

```
def new(quiz_fields) do
  QuizValidator.errors(quiz_fields)
  |> case do
    {:error, message} ->
      {:error, message}
    _ ->
      QuizManager.build_quiz(quiz_fields)
  end
end
```

This function is relatively small, but the service layers must often compose across more steps. When each individual step has its own error condition, you'll have to nest these case statements each time you deal with a separate error. Any notion that you're dealing with a composition is completely lost.

The solution is to use with to build the composition, like this:

```
def new(quiz_fields) do
  with :ok <- QuizValidator.errors(quiz_fields) do
    QuizManager.build_quiz(quiz_fields)
  end
end
```

The with function does two things for us. It allows us to compose through the "happy path" of the code by letting us delay error handling. with also lets us clearly separate what to do if the composition succeeds or fails.

Now that we have a couple of strategies for dealing with errors, let's start to work on our own boundary layer. Remember, the first part of winning the boundary game is deciding whether to play.

Build Your Optional Server

One of the trickiest parts of learning a concurrency-based language like Elixir is understanding when to use processes at all. Here's a little guidance. Consider processes when these use cases show up:

- Sharing state across processes

- Presenting a uniform API for external services such as databases or communications

- Managing side effects such as logging or file I/O

- Monitoring system-wide resources or performance metrics

- Isolating critical services from failure

This short list is not exhaustive, but it should give you a sense for the types of things that should prompt you to think about a boundary. In short, our boundary is an *optional* layer of *impure integration code* that make the core *fast, robust, and reliable.*

For our Mastery project, a couple of those use cases ring true. We will need to *share data* across two types of state including a repository of quizzes as well as the data for an individual quiz session. We also want to *isolate failure* because our overall quiz repository is a critical system and a single point of failure. If it fails, no one will be taking any quizzes!

Now that we've decided to use processes, we can decide whether to use our own machinery or to rely on other infrastructure. We might choose the Phoenix web server because it already has excellent process infrastructure. In our case, we'd like to preserve the freedom to provide other types of user interfaces beyond the web, such as a possible native user interface, so we'll go ahead and flesh out our boundary layer.

Let's look back at an example. In Chapter 1, Build Your Project in Layers, on page 1, recall our simple counter that wrapped a tiny core with processes and recursion to manage state. That wrapper is our *service layer*. We then took that ad hoc server and wrapped it in an API. This last layer exists as a convenience.

We're going to follow the same pattern. Think about the boundary in two parts: the service layer and the API layer. A boundary needs a service layer around each individual process type and an external API for clean, direct access across services. In Mastery, we'll first need to decide what our GenServers are. We'll need a service layer for each of two GenServers: a quiz session where users can take a quiz and a quiz manager where we'll hold the state for individual quizzes. Then we'll put an API, like this:

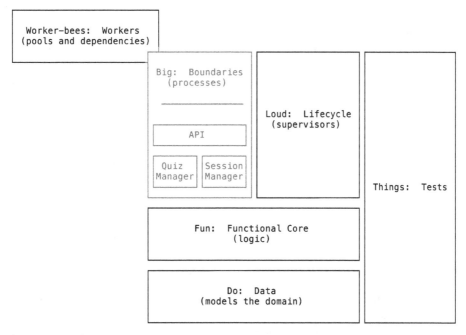

This figure illustrates the story nicely. Our QuizManager and SessionManager will be separate services and we'll tie them together with a unified API.

The OTP framework is pretty expansive. We'll work primarily with GenServers, a short name for *generic server*. It's the most basic OTP abstraction with the features most users need. The original documentation says you will use GenServers to establish a client–server relationship. You can use them to write state machines, build process-based services such as web servers, or even share common, independent state. Your main three APIs will be init/1, handle_call/3 and handle_cast/2. You'll use them this way.

init(initial_state) will establish the state of a new GenServer. Indirectly we'll invoke initial_state each time we start a server. More precisely, it comes from the supervisor, which we'll explore in more detail in Chapter 7, Customize Your Lifecycle, on page 131. It returns a tuple that looks like {:ok, initial_state}.

handle_call(message, from, state) processes a synchronous two-way message. Think phone *call* because phone calls are two way. When your code sends a GenServer a call message, OTP will invoke the handle_call callback with the message, a tuple describing the caller, and the current state of the server. Then, your handle_call callback returns a value in a predetermined format. For example, to reply, use {:reply, message_to_client, new_state}. The GenServer sends the value message_to_client to the client process, and sets the new value of the GenServer to new_state with a recursive function call.

handle_cast(message, state) processes a one-way asynchronous message. Think pod *cast* because podcasts are one way. You'll sometimes use cast messages as a fire-and-forget mechanism to change state. A cast will typically respond with a {:noreply, new_state} tuple to change the server's state to new_state. There are other callbacks and specialized responses you can find in the documentation, but that's all of the background we need to write a basic server API.

The main decision we need to make to start with is which servers we'll need. Intuitively, we'll need two of them. One server will handle all of the quizzes as users create and store them, and another server will let each user take a quiz. That strategy makes sense because many users could take each quiz, and each will need their own process because each has its own state. We only need one server to hold our collection of quizzes. Let's make it so.

Implement the QuizManager with Processes

The quiz manager will start with an empty map. We'll add quizzes to it through a call to :build_quiz. Then, we'll add templates to a quiz in the store through a call to :add_template, and we'll add a function to let our users lookup a quiz by name.

Open a new editor session in lib/mastery/boundary/quiz_manager.ex. It's a straight Elixir module that looks like this:

Boundary/lib/mastery/boundary/quiz_manager.ex

```
defmodule Mastery.Boundary.QuizManager do
  alias Mastery.Core.Quiz
  use GenServer
```

We declare the module, set up our initial aliases for Quiz. Then we use GenServer. use is an Elixir macro. As you know, macros are code that writes code. This one adds the GenServer callbacks our component will need, and some machinery the server needs to run that we don't need to worry about quite yet.

The first order of business is to establish an external API for our GenServer:

```
Boundary/lib/mastery/boundary/quiz_manager.ex
def init(quizzes) when is_map(quizzes) do
  {:ok, quizzes}
end

def init(_quizzes), do: {:error, "quizzes must be a map"}
```

Next is the simple init callback to initialize our server. That callback takes some inbound arguments and translates those to an initial state for our server. We want the initial state for for QuizManager to be a map called quizzes. If it's not a map, we'll return a descriptive error.

Let's write our first call callback, the one to build a quiz:

```
Boundary/lib/mastery/boundary/quiz_manager.ex
def handle_call({:build_quiz, quiz_fields}, _from, quizzes) do
  quiz = Quiz.new(quiz_fields)
  new_quizzes = Map.put(quizzes, quiz.title, quiz)
  {:reply, :ok, new_quizzes}
end
```

This is our first handle_call *callback*. We use the word "callback" because a GenServer implements all of the boilerplate for a generic server, including a recursive loop to manage state. The generic implementation has a few hooks that let users fill in the project-specific knowledge. In our case, our callback builds and stores a quiz.

OTP invokes handle_call whenever our GenServer receives a call message. Rather than handling all messages from one function, we'll generally break up the handle_call endpoints with pattern matching so we can keep each message in its own function block.

This call takes the form {:build_quiz, quiz_fields}. The work is simple: we call our functional core to create a new quiz from these fields, and then add that quiz to our map.

When we're done, we return a three-tuple. The first one instructs OTP to send a reply to the user, the second has the value for the reply, and the third is the new state for the GenServer, in our case the map new_quizzes containing our new quiz.

That first call is a little tricky, but the rest will look the same. Let's add a template, like this:

Boundary/lib/mastery/boundary/quiz_manager.ex
```
def handle_call(
  {:add_template, quiz_title, template_fields},
  _from,
  quizzes
) do
  new_quizzes = Map.update!(quizzes, quiz_title, fn quiz ->
    Quiz.add_template(quiz, template_fields)
  end)
  {:reply, :ok, new_quizzes}
end
```

This callback uses the same technique to add templates to a quiz. We invoke Quiz.add_template from our core and store that result to our map using Map.update. We return :ok to the user and set the new server state to new_quizzes.

Now that we can add quizzes with templates to our simple store, let's support fetches:

Boundary/lib/mastery/boundary/quiz_manager.ex
```
  def handle_call({:lookup_quiz_by_title, quiz_title}, _from, quizzes) do

    {:reply, quizzes[quiz_title], quizzes}
  end
end
```

This final call looks up a quiz and returns it to the user. It's a trivial Map.get.

We now have all of the machinery we need, but we could surface a cleaner API. Let's add more convenient functions to use that callback, like this:

Boundary/lib/mastery/boundary/quiz_manager.ex
```
def build_quiz(manager \\ __MODULE__, quiz_fields) do
  GenServer.call(manager, {:build_quiz, quiz_fields})
end

def add_template(manager \\ __MODULE__, quiz_title, template_fields) do
  GenServer.call(manager, {:add_template, quiz_title, template_fields})
end

def lookup_quiz_by_title(manager \\ __MODULE__, quiz_title) do
  GenServer.call(manager, {:lookup_quiz_by_title, quiz_title})
end
```

Notice that most of the machinery for GenServer is pretty compact, but it provides too many implementation details. We leak through the exact format of each call message, unnecessarily coupling our GenServer to any code that invokes it. We provide a cleaner API with these three client functions.

In this layer, you can see the consumer side of the GenServer module. For each of the messages in our API, we call a GenServer.call function to send a message. We first pass the name of the GenServer which we'll default to the module name, then the message we're sending. The message we send will match one of the handle_call function clauses in our server. We expect clients to invoke these three APIs and the handle_call callbacks to run on the server.

Now that we're done, users can interact with our server with plain old functions rather than messages, and we've sufficiently hidden the details of each message. Let's take this server for a test drive.

Try the Quiz Manager

In this section, we're going to put the quiz through its paces. Part of writing good code is building the infrastructure to support learning and exploration. We're going to create a trivial module to let new users and developers alike explore our features in the console.

Let's create a simple math quiz with mastery of two and a template for single-digit addition. None of this code will be new to you:

```
Boundary/lib/mastery/examples/math.ex
defmodule Mastery.Examples.Math do
  alias Mastery.Core.Quiz
  def template_fields() do
    [
      name: :single_digit_addition,
      category: :addition,
      instructions: "Add the numbers",
      raw: "<%= @left %> + <%= @right %>",
      generators: addition_generators(),
      checker: &addition_checker/2
    ]
  end

  def addition_checker(substitutions, answer) do
    left = Keyword.fetch!(substitutions, :left)
    right = Keyword.fetch!(substitutions, :right)
    to_string(left + right) == String.trim(answer)
  end

  def addition_generators() do
    %{left: Enum.to_list(0..9), right: Enum.to_list(0..9)}
  end

  def quiz_fields() do
    %{ mastery: 2, title: :simple_addition}
  end
```

```
def quiz() do
    quiz_fields()
    |> Quiz.new
    |> Quiz.add_template(template_fields())
  end
end
```

We have separate functions for quiz and template fields. We also have a function to roll that up into a new quiz. Now we have a few tools that will make our module easy to test. Open up a new IEx session, or at least recompile. Then, you can alias the modules we'll need, like this:

```
iex(1)> alias Mastery.Examples.Math
Mastery.Examples.Math
iex(2)> alias Mastery.Boundary.QuizManager
Mastery.Boundary.QuizManager
```

We alias Math, the example quiz we just built for convenience, and QuizManager, the server layer for building quizzes. Now, we need to start the quiz:

```
iex(3)> GenServer.start_link QuizManager, %{}, name: QuizManager
{:ok, #PID<0.123.0>}
```

We need to be able to access our server, perhaps from a web layer so we'll need to be able to reference it by name. We'll use the name of the module, which means we'll only have one copy of QuizManager. The start_link has three arguments, the module that has the GenServer implementation, the empty map that will eventually contain our quizzes, and options. We use the :name option to specify the name for our new server. Now, we can use it:

```
iex(4)> QuizManager.build_quiz title: :quiz
:ok
iex(5)> QuizManager.add_template :quiz, Math.template_fields
:ok
```

You can see the smoother API we offer from this layer. We build a quiz, strictly with functions:

```
iex(6)> QuizManager.lookup_quiz_by_title :quiz
%Mastery.Core.Quiz{ ... }
```

Nice! That much works. We can see the individual fields of the quiz we added. That's more than half of our server. Now admin users can establish new quizzes. It's time to switch to the rest of our server layer, the part for taking quizzes and answering questions.

Implement the QuizSession with Processes

The quiz session will use the code we implemented in our functional core, the code that answers and selects questions for a given user. Our core implements the business functions that advance the state of the quiz based on mastery. The quiz session will add the process machinery we'll need to independently manage state.

Each of our users will need the state for the quiz they're working through as well as their own email address for their answers. The state for our GenServer will be a tuple with quiz email.

For now, we won't worry about starting and stopping that server. We'll just make sure it works with a single process. Let's start with the quiz session. Open the new file lib/mastery/boundary/quiz_session.ex, and key this in:

```
Boundary/lib/mastery/boundary/quiz_session.ex
defmodule Mastery.Boundary.QuizSession do
  alias Mastery.Core.{Quiz, Response}
  use GenServer
```

We declare the module, set up our initial aliases for Quiz and Response. Once again we use GenServer.

Next, let's write a simple callback to initialize our server and our first callback, like this:

```
Boundary/lib/mastery/boundary/quiz_session.ex
def init({quiz, email}) do
  {:ok, {quiz, email}}
end
```

This init function looks like the first one we coded. We take the expected {quiz, email} tuple and return it to our server. We don't validate here, except making sure we're using the API in the right way with an inbound tuple. We'll check data integrity at the API layer.

Next, let's process a callback to select a question, like this:

```
Boundary/lib/mastery/boundary/quiz_session.ex
def handle_call(:select_question, _from, {quiz, email}) do
  quiz = Quiz.select_question(quiz)
  {:reply, quiz.current_question.asked, {quiz, email}}
end
```

The task is complex, but we already handled the difficult part in the functional core. This callback just calls that layer directly, and formats the :reply tuple. We return the question to ask the user, and set our {quiz, email} tuple.

Now, a user can start a quiz with a start_link and a call to :select_question. What remains is to answer a question, like this:

Boundary/lib/mastery/boundary/quiz_session.ex
```
  def handle_call({:answer_question, answer}, _from, {quiz, email}) do
    quiz
    |> Quiz.answer_question(Response.new(quiz, email, answer))
    |> Quiz.select_question
    |> maybe_finish(email)
  end

  defp maybe_finish(nil, _email), do: {:stop, :normal, :finished, nil}
  defp maybe_finish(quiz, email) do
    {
      :reply,
      {quiz.current_question.asked, quiz.last_response.correct},
      {quiz, email}
    }
  end
end
```

This function calls answer_question to answer the question and then advances the quiz. It returns the presentation data that we will need later to show to the user: the question text and whether the answer is right or wrong.

This is the first handle_call that has significant logic in it, a pattern match to a private function called maybe_finish. The logic actually belongs in the server layer because it interprets the select_question response. When a quiz is through, it is set to nil.

Our first maybe_finish clause does a lot of heavy lifting in a tiny amount of code. By replying with a :stop tuple, we can tell the GenServer how to terminate and what to send to the user, and the new state for the server. We want a :normal termination, :finished goes to the user and the server gets nil as the new state.

If the quiz is not nil, we return the question.asked text and response.correct so the user knows the next question and whether the previous question was right or wrong.

Now we have the bare-metal GenServer, but we still need to wrap up our external API. That's easy since there are only two functions to provide, like this:

Boundary/lib/mastery/boundary/quiz_session.ex
```
def select_question(session) do
  GenServer.call(session, :select_question)
end

def answer_question(session, answer) do
  GenServer.call(session, {:answer_question, answer})
end
```

We're processing two call functions, one to call :select_question and one to call :answer_question. The concepts are exactly the same as the client functions we added to the QuizManager server. It's complete, and we can take it for a spin.

Test Drive the Quiz Session

We will connect to our server with the GenServer module and the various functions we've built in the QuizManager module. Open up IEx with iex -S mix or use recompile in your existing session. We'll want to set up the aliases and start up the server:

```
iex(1)> alias Mastery.Boundary.QuizSession
Mastery.Boundary.QuizSession
iex(2)> alias Mastery.Examples.Math
Mastery.Examples.Math
```

We alias the two modules we need, the Math example quiz and the QuizSession server layer. Next, it's an easy step to spin up a QuizSession process with a GenServer.start_link, like this:

```
iex(3)> {:ok, session} = \
  GenServer.start_link  QuizSession, {Math.quiz(), "mathy@example.com"}
{:ok, #PID<0.114.0>}
```

Having the Math.quiz function ready to go made this easy. We started a QuizSession GenServer with a quiz and email address, to match the QuizSession.init/1 function we coded earlier. We got an :ok tuple, so we're ready to proceed.

This time, we'll need the session value; it contains our pid:

```
iex(4)> QuizSession.select_question session
"0 + 4"
```

We call our GenServer's client API to select_question, providing our session, and it picked a question for us. Now, we can answer a couple of questions right twice in a row and finish our quiz as masters of the universe, or at least masters of single-digit addition, like this:

```
iex(5)> QuizSession.answer_question session, "4"
{"2 + 8", true}
iex(6)> QuizSession.answer_question session, "10"
:finished
```

Marvelous! We answer two questions correctly in a row. The first time, the QuizSession returns the question text and true, meaning we got the previous question right. After two successive right answers, we have mastery and the quiz is finished.

The GenServer API works, but we still have a little work to do. So far, our servers have isolated client APIs which only do isolated jobs, and with potentially corrupt user data. We'll also need a layer to stitch together the two concepts of making a quiz and taking the quiz. We'll do that work now.

Wrap the Server in an API

The API layer's job is to insulate the server layer from inconsistent data and to stitch together independent concepts from the individual GenServer implementations. It will also hide internal implementations from the user, such as the Quiz struct we make available from our QuizManager server. Any implementation details from server layers or the functional cores will be off limits.

Though our internal details may be radically different, the API-wrapped server will share many characteristics of an OOP object. It will hide implementation details, including state, behind an API of functions. It will allow complex interactions between components with message passing, and will allow convenient state tracking.

Before we dive into the API, we'll need some validations that assist us in our work. Let's do that now.

Build Validations

For validations, we want to pick the *closest common access point* to the user. Right now, we're imagining a quiz as service that can run without persistence, say on an educational website or as a database-backed quiz engine in a more formal classroom setting. In either case, we want to keep the code in our server clean, and implement validations exactly once. Given those constraints, we will validate at the API level.

Our strategy for building validations is simple. Each validator, whether it works with a nested list or a simple field with a single validator, must reduce over a list of errors. These errors serve as an accumulator. If the errors are empty after fully validating each field, then the model is valid.

We could use changesets, but introducing changesets brings all of Ecto along with them, at least as we write this. Rather than introduce database concepts to a stateless layer, we'll build a rough feature to do the work. It's a surprisingly easy task.

Rough Out Generic Tools

Let's start with a validation library with a couple of useful common functions. We'll start with the require function to validate all required fields and an optional function, in lib/mastery/boundary/validator.ex like this:

Boundary/lib/mastery/boundary/validator.ex
```elixir
defmodule Mastery.Boundary.Validator do
  def require(errors, fields, field_name, validator) do
    present = Map.has_key?(fields, field_name)
    check_required_field(present, fields, errors, field_name, validator)
  end

  def optional(errors, fields, field_name, validator) do
    if Map.has_key?(fields, field_name) do
      require(errors, fields, field_name, validator)
    else
      errors
    end
  end
end
```

For both required and optional fields, we check to see if a field is present. We pass the present through to the underlying check_required_field. It may seem strange to pass optional fields through to this function, but if you think about it, optional and required fields that are present behave exactly the same way.

Let's look at a quick convenience function, check:

Boundary/lib/mastery/boundary/validator.ex
```elixir
def check(true=_valid, _message), do: :ok
def check(false=_valid, message), do: message
```

This function just adds a little sugar to custom validations. Each check request first makes some type of conditional test, indicating whether the field is valid. If it is, we return :ok. If not we return the supplied tuple. This trivial function will lighten up the individual validators considerably.

Now, let's look at the functions that do the physical generic validations. First, let's look at the check_required_field function that looks like this:

Boundary/lib/mastery/boundary/validator.ex
```elixir
defp check_required_field(true=_present, fields, errors, field_name, f) do
  valid = fields |> Map.fetch!(field_name) |> f.()
  check_field(valid, errors, field_name)
end
defp check_required_field(_present, _fields, errors, field_name, _f) do
  errors ++ [{field_name, "is required"}]
end
```

```elixir
  defp check_field(:ok, _errors, _field_name), do: :ok
  defp check_field({:error, message}, errors, field_name) do
    errors ++ [{field_name, message}]
  end
  defp check_field({:errors, messages}, errors, field_name) do
    errors ++ Enum.map(messages, &{field_name, &1})
  end
end
```

If a function is present, we just fire the underlying validator, passing the result through to check_field. If not, we add a {field_name, "is required"} tuple to the list of errors.

Since we've already fired the validation function, check_field is surprisingly lean. It needs only match against expected results, which may be a single error, multiple errors, or :ok. In either error case, we add the errors to the list of errors and continue until all fields are validated. Now we can put these tools to work.

Validate Quizzes

We first need to validate a quiz. We are creating a module per validator, and we only add models that take complex user data. In lib/mastery/boundary/quiz_validator.ex, write this code:

Boundary/lib/mastery/boundary/quiz_validator.ex
```elixir
defmodule Mastery.Boundary.QuizValidator do
  import Mastery.Boundary.Validator

  def errors(fields) when is_map(fields) do
    [ ]
    |> require(fields, :title, &validate_title/1)
    |> optional(fields, :mastery, &validate_mastery/1)
  end
  def errors(_fields), do: [{nil, "A map of fields is required"}]
```

We have a core errors function that does the lion's share of the work. We have only two fields that have external input, an optional :mastery field and a required :title field. We pipe through those, and return the responses. Now let's work on the individual fields:

Boundary/lib/mastery/boundary/quiz_validator.ex
```elixir
  def validate_title(title) when is_binary(title) do
    check(String.match?(title, ~r{\S}), {:error, "can't be blank"})
  end
  def validate_title(_title), do: {:error, "must be a string"}

  def validate_mastery(mastery) when is_integer(mastery) do
    check(mastery >= 1, {:error, "must be greater than zero"})
  end
  def validate_mastery(_mastery), do: {:error, "must be an integer"}
end
```

Elixir's pattern matching and our check function makes individual validations strikingly simple. We first match on the datatype and then call check to do individual checks. Then, we add a catchall for other datatypes and return an appropriate error.

With the simplest validation out of the way, we can shift to the trickier validation layer, templates. It's a little tricker because it has some complex datatypes like functions and lists of generators. Let's see how we can structure those concepts next.

Validate Templates

The template fields represent a sterner test. The checker and generators fields will require us to validate lists and functions. Still, our simple framework that's based on composition will make quick work of them.

Let's start with the basic errors function that composes validations over each field. As before, we'll enumerate required and optional fields, in lib/mastery/boundary/template_validator.ex, like this:

```
Boundary/lib/mastery/boundary/template_validator.ex
defmodule Mastery.Boundary.TemplateValidator do
  import Mastery.Boundary.Validator

  def errors(fields) when is_list(fields) do
    fields = Map.new(fields)
    [ ]
    |> require(fields, :name, &validate_name/1)
    |> require(fields, :category, &validate_name/1)
    |> optional(fields, :instructions, &validate_instructions/1)
    |> require(fields, :raw, &validate_raw/1)
    |> require(fields, :generators, &validate_generators/1)
    |> require(fields, :checker, &validate_checker/1)
  end
  def errors(_fields), do: [{nil, "A keyword list of fields is required"}]
```

The technique works exactly as it did in the QuizValidator. Now, let's work on the individual fields. These are the easy ones:

```
Boundary/lib/mastery/boundary/template_validator.ex
def validate_name(name) when is_atom(name), do: :ok
def validate_name(_name), do: {:error, "must be an atom"}

def validate_instructions(instructions) when is_binary(instructions), do: :ok
def validate_instructions(_instructions), do: {:error, "must be a binary"}

def validate_raw(raw) when is_binary(raw) do
  check(String.match?(raw, ~r{\S}), {:error, "can't be blank"})
end
def validate_raw(_raw), do: {:error, "must be a string"}
```

The :name, :raw and :instructions fields work exactly as they did in QuizValidator. We use a combination of pattern matching and the check function to do all of the validation we need. Let's see if our concepts extend to the generators and checkers:

```
Boundary/lib/mastery/boundary/template_validator.ex
def validate_generators(generators) when is_map(generators) do
  generators
  |> Enum.map(&validate_generator/1)
  |> Enum.reject(&(&1 == :ok))
  |> case do
    [ ] ->
      :ok
    errors ->
      {:errors, errors}
  end
end
def validate_generators(_generators), do: {:error, "must be a map"}
```

Recall that we're leaning on the composition of our validators. You can see the benefits of this approach as we validate all generators. To validate the list, we map over the list of generators, validating each one and filtering out the :ok results. If the whole list is empty, we return :ok; otherwise, we return the errors.

That code is complex, but our composition strategy does not break down. We're almost done. Let's validate the individual generators, like this:

```
Boundary/lib/mastery/boundary/template_validator.ex
  def validate_generator({name, generator})
  when is_atom(name) and is_list(generator) do
    check(generator != [ ], {:error, "can't be empty"})
  end
  def validate_generator({name, generator})
  when is_atom(name) and is_function(generator, 0) do
    :ok
  end
  def validate_generator(_generator),
    do: {:error, "must be a string to list or function pair"}

  def validate_checker(checker) when is_function(checker, 2), do: :ok
  def validate_checker(_checker), do: {:error, "must be an arity 2 function"}
end
```

To validate a single generator, we use pattern matching and guards to make sure that:

- The generator list is not empty
- The generator is a two-tuple with an atom as a name and a function of the form &generator/0.

If so we return :ok; if not we return an error tuple. And we're done. We built our own validations and it was not nearly as complicated as you might have guessed. Our validator is easy to extend and each specialized validator implements a single update scenario, much like Ecto changesets.

With the validations out of the way, it's time to push out beyond the server layer. It's time to build the API. We'll finally remove the hello world code and use the mastery.ex file. Let's make it happen.

Build the API Layer

Our API layer will name the concepts of the GenServer and also smooth out some of the rough edges. We'll build a lightweight API that uses the GenServer module to do starts, calls, and casts. The first step is to do the typical imports we need. In lib/mastery.ex we'll delete the default implementation and set up the aliases we need:

```
Boundary/lib/mastery.ex
defmodule Mastery do
  alias Mastery.Boundary.{QuizSession, QuizManager}
  alias Mastery.Boundary.{TemplateValidator, QuizValidator}
  alias Mastery.Core.Quiz
```

If possible, we'd like to build a service layer where the only functions we need are in the service layer. Unfortunately, we also have to manage the validations, so we'll add those aliases as well. We also need to alias the Core.Quiz module to pass that data between the QuizManager and QuizSession modules. This is the right place to do that job because this layer exists to stitch together these disparate concepts. The main thing is to keep the API layer as thin as possible, and take on as little of the business logic as we can.

Validation belongs here because we want to reduce the need for dealing with the uncertainty of the outside world from the API layer as we can.

Our first job is to kick off the manager, like this:

```
Boundary/lib/mastery.ex
def start_quiz_manager() do
  GenServer.start_link(QuizManager, %{}, name: QuizManager)
end
```

The GenServer.start_link does the heavy lifting. We need to name the server so that in the event of a crash, we'll be able to find it again. Since we'll only ever need one, we'll name it after the module. You may have noticed we defaulted our client APIs to use the module name as well, so we'll be able to keep the ceremony in this layer low.

Now, let's build a quiz:

Boundary/lib/mastery.ex
```
def build_quiz(fields) do
  with :ok <- QuizValidator.errors(fields),
       :ok <-GenServer.call(QuizManager, {:build_quiz, fields}),
  do: :ok, else: (error -> error)
end
```

The real work starts when we add a quiz. Now, we have imperfect user data that we need to validate. Earlier, we learned that composition with pipes is elegant and beautiful, but pipes do not deal well with the midstream errors we're dealing with in this example.

To solve that problem, instead of pipes we use with to validate the fields and do a GenServer call to :build_quiz. Notice we use a one-line syntax for the do: :ok, else: (error -> error) clauses. We do this *strictly because we are passing values straight through.* We don't want to distract from the purpose of this function, which is the composition of the actions in the first clause.

We'll use a similar technique to add the templates:

Boundary/lib/mastery.ex
```
def add_template(title, fields) do
  with :ok <- TemplateValidator.errors(fields),
       :ok <- GenServer.call(QuizManager, {:add_template, title, fields}),
  do: :ok, else: (error -> error)
end
```

We compose two functions with with, one to validate the templates and the second to invoke our server layer with GenServer.call.

With that, the QuizManager has set up the quiz and can pass the baton to the QuizSession server:

Boundary/lib/mastery.ex
```
def take_quiz(title, email) do
  with %Quiz{}=quiz <- QuizManager.lookup_quiz_by_title(title),
       {:ok, session} <- GenServer.start_link(QuizSession, {quiz, email})
  do
    session
  else
    error -> error
  end
end
```

This code does the handoff from one system to the next. The take_quiz function first looks up a quiz and then uses a GenServer.start_link to create a new server with that quiz and an email. We return the session pid so other functions can call it later.

Next, we build a function each to select a question, like this:

```
Boundary/lib/mastery.ex
  def select_question(session) do
    GenServer.call(session, :select_question)
  end

  def answer_question(session, answer) do
    GenServer.call(session, {:answer_question, answer})
  end
end
```

They are straight calls to GenServer, with no intervening logic. That's about as thin a layer around a GenServer as we could hope to have. The API is easy to understand and about as easy as it could be to use.

The layer may seem unnecessary, but it's not. This API layer is the first point of access for developers investigating our function. A simple API layer that handles only external concerns is the secret to good client–server design. Presenting a public-facing API makes it crystal clear that changes to these functions comes at a cost.

It's also an anchor point for public-facing ceremony. If we were to build documentation, this file is where it would go. It's the first place we would add type specs, module docs, and the like.

Our goal is to make the maintenance on the borders between APIs *explicit*. The secret to doing so is decoupling. Let's see how we did. Our first test of this public interface will be an in-console session.

Test Drive the API

This exercise is the culmination of everything we've done in the boundary layer. We'll roll up all the work we've done so far. This quiz flow will depend on the data structures we defined and make use of the functions we established in the functional core.

The service layers will use that functional core to track state in two pieces, the quiz maker we call the manager and the quiz taker we call the session. We'll use the client APIs from those GenServers that hide those details. We won't see the shapes of internal call or cast messages. All of the data flowing out of the API will be pure Elixir data structures, with no custom structs. Aside from lifecycle details, this layer will show data exactly as we'll present it to the outside world.

Rev up iex -S mix. If you've left it open from last time you'll need to issue the recompile command. Then we can start to use our API:

```
iex(1)> alias Mastery.Examples.Math
Mastery.Examples.Math
```

Notice that the only piece of information we need to alias is the Math module that has the raw data we'll use to create a quiz. That's a good sign. We really don't need anything else to use our API because none of the inner details are exposed.

Let's fire up the manager and create a quiz, like this:

```
iex(2)> Mastery.start_quiz_manager
{:ok, #PID<0.113.0>}
iex(3)> Mastery.build_quiz Math.quiz_fields
:ok
iex(4)> Mastery.add_template Math.quiz.title, Math.template_fields
:ok
```

With the example data, establishing a new quiz with exactly what we need is trivial. We build a quiz and add a template.

Now we can take a quiz, like this:

```
iex(5)> session = Mastery.take_quiz Math.quiz.title, "mathy@email.com"
#PID<0.117.0>
iex(6)> Mastery.select_question session
"8 + 7"
```

We get the session, which is a pid, and use it to select the first question:

```
iex(7)> Mastery.answer_question session, "wrong"
{"9 + 5", false}
iex(8)> Mastery.answer_question session, "14"
{"0 + 2", true}
iex(9)> Mastery.answer_question session, "2"
:finished
```

We get the first answer wrong. With a mastery of two and a single template, we need only get two consecutive questions correct to finish the quiz. We can tell that the process is dead, like this:

```
iex(10)> Process.alive? session
false
```

Boom. The server is stopped, as it should be. In all, we've done good work. We're using the top-level Mastery module as it should be, and the concepts are well named. We don't have to worry about sending messages. We just call functions.

Now that the service layer is in, let's review some of the main decisions we made. You might have noticed that we used call several times when we returned an :ok value. You might be wondering why we chose not to use cast messages instead. The answer is not as simple as it may seem on the surface. Let's find out why.

Prefer Call Over Cast to Provide Back Pressure

Intuitively, you might think that it's best to use the one-way handle_cast to send messages that don't need responses. For example, the :add_template message doesn't really need a response. We just trust that the template was added successfully. If it's not, something has gone horribly wrong. There's nothing we can do beyond crashing the server and reporting the reasons for the crash back to the user.

Interestingly, handle_cast is rarely the best option for sending messages. In this section, we'll look at one of the reasons why. They are called serializability and back pressure. Let's explore why.

As you probably know, each Elixir process has a message queue. We'll call it the mailbox. Unlike a physical mailbox, Elixir processes only receive messages from it; they don't send from the mailbox. Like a true mailbox, if the receiving process for a given message is struggling, the mailbox can overflow, often leading to severe problems that are hard to debug.

A good example is the Elixir logger. If your production code is sending log messages quicker than the logger can handle them, either because the sender is logging too many log requests or because the logger's disk I/O is somehow compromised, we don't want the logger to immediately stop logging messages.

The Elixir logger has an excellent solution for this problem. It's called selective back-pressure. That means that when the logger gets into trouble, it will detect this problem and start slowing the clients down by switching from cast to call.

Making the logger's client wait for every request to finish before sending the next one relieves the pressure on the logger itself by slowing down the flow of messages. If the logger still can't keep up, it announces this failure as a log message and begins to discard messages until the logger gets to a more manageable threshold.

Let's dive into some specific details. We'll start with configuration.

Users can configure options to represent thresholds. These thresholds specify when a healthy logger becomes sick because its message logger gets too long.

Two of these thresholds specify when to go from cast to call, or when to start shedding messages.

Users can also configure thresholds defining when the system goes from sick to healthy. When an unhealthy system has a message queue that shrinks below these thresholds, the logger can stop discarding messages, or go back to cast from call.

The logger code then uses that configuration to implement three different modes to implement the cast, call and shedding modes. They are called :async, :sync, and :discard, respectively.

Now, let's look at the specific Elixir implementation. As a general metric for system health, sometimes it helps to look at the number of messages in a processes mail box. Here's the code that does that job:

```elixir
defp message_queue_length() do
  {:message_queue_len, messages} = Process.info(self(), :message_queue_len)
  messages
end
```

Process.info(self(), :message_queue_length) does the magic. It returns an integer value that is the number of messages in the queue. The logger can then make use of it.

Now we can see how the logger switches modes. In logger/config.ex, the logger computes the right mode, like this:

```elixir
case mode do
  _ when messages >= discard_threshold -> :discard
  :discard when messages > keep_threshold -> :discard
  _ when messages >= sync_threshold -> :sync
  :sync when messages > async_threshold -> :sync
  _ -> :async
end
```

This snippet computes the mode given the message queue length in messages. The thresholds in this function all come from the logger configuration. These thresholds work in pairs. One threshold in each pair marks the transition from healthy to sick, and one marks the transition from sick to healthy.

We shed messages if the function is greater than discard_threshold; we stay in discard mode if we stay above the keep_threshold. Otherwise, we switch to sync mode if we are over the sync_threshold, and stay in that mode if it's already in sync mode and the messages are above the async_threshold. If none of those things are true, we're healthy, so we send async.

Now, we can compare the configured mode with the computed one, like this:

```
def handle_event(_event, {state, thresholds}) do
    %{mode: mode} = state

case compute_mode(mode, thresholds) do
^mode ->
  {:ok, {state, thresholds}}
```

If the mode matches the mode that was configured, do nothing. Otherwise:

```
new_mode ->
  if new_mode == :discard do
    message =
      "Logger has #{message_queue_length()} messages in its queue, " <>
        "which is above :discard_threshold. Messages will be discarded " <>
        "until the message queue goes back to 75% of the threshold size"

    log(:warn, message, state)
  end

  if mode == :discard do
    log(:warn, "Logger has stopped discarding messages", state)
  end
```

If things are very bad and we're beyond the discard limit, we set the :discard state so we can shed messages until we're healthy. We log a message to tell the user we're no longer logging, pending improvements.

All that remains is to set the new mode in the logger, like this:

```
    state = persist(%{state | mode: new_mode})
    {:ok, {state, thresholds}}
end
```

We set the new mode and let the logger lose. Let's see :discard in action.

```
def __should_log__(level) when level in @levels do
  ...
  if compare_levels(level, min_level) != :lt and mode != :discard do
    {level, config, pdict}
  else
    :error
  end
  ...
end
```

In a function called _should_log_ we check the mode for :discard. If it's set, regardless of log level, we'll return :error.

In *logger.ex*, the bare log looks like this:

```
def bare_log(level, chardata_or_fun, metadata \\ []) do
  case __should_log__(level) do
    :error -> :ok
    info -> __do_log__(info, chardata_or_fun, metadata)
  end
end
```

If the mode is :error, we do nothing, shedding the messages. Otherwise we call *do_log*, a long function which eventually does this:

```
notify(mode, {level, Process.group_leader(), tuple})
```

We're finally at the magic moment. We choose call or cast to handle back pressure. At the very bottom of *logger.ex*, you'll see these functions:

```
defp notify(:sync, msg), do: :gen_event.sync_notify(Logger, msg)
defp notify(:async, msg), do: :gen_event.notify(Logger, msg)
```

This means Elixir will log messages as a call (sync) or cast (async).

Here's the point. If your code uses handle_call instead of handle_cast, you don't need to worry as much because you can only send messages as fast as your server can process them. It's a great automatic governor on a server.

Rarely, you'll want to use cast messages to start multiple workers at once, or to notify multiple workers simultaneously. Try to be judicious with this approach, though.

Back pressure is one reason to avoid cast messages. It's not the only reason, though. Let's look at the next one.

Extend Your APIs Safely

So far, we've strongly advocated building many small components and managing those components through dependencies. When this strategy is working well, it simplifies your job by limiting the scope of what you need to understand to make any given change.

This strategy can go to a special hell fueled by cascading dependencies in a hurry, if you're not careful with how you build your APIs. Specifically, maintaining a healthy ecosystem is difficult if each release of an API breaks compatibility to old versions of the API. Breaking changes have several different forms:

- An API can add requirements to input parameters such as adding a new required field to our Quiz.

- An API can change the shape of the output such as changing all of our quiz functions to {:ok, quiz}.

- An API can change their behavior in unexpected ways such as treating an amount as dollars rather than cents.

Let's look quickly at an approach to APIs that will improve compatibility as you improve the various independent components in your system. We'll honor three rules.

Don't Add New Requirements to Existing APIs, Only Options

Many beginning developers tend to validate all arguments for a remote API. Then, as those APIs need to be extended, they require those as well. There's a problem with that approach.

If servers provide requests that require all parameters, each new parameter means you'll have to upgrade the client and server simultaneously. With just one client and one server component, that strategy may seem viable but as dependencies like this cascade through a system, upgrades get exponentially more difficult. Then, you lose all of the advantages you were seeking by building decoupled components in the first place.

If you want to extend an API, extend it with options. Then, servers can provide new API functionality to the same endpoints without requiring all clients to change. Later, clients can upgrade to take advantage of these new options.

Ignore Anything You Don't Understand

The "no new requirements" rule pertains to public-facing APIs. There's a similar rule for dealing with data. Ignoring everything you don't understand makes it possible to slowly add new fields, request options that may not yet be supported, and to upgrade your systems incrementally.

These first two rules work together well. For example, say there's an export program that's expecting a fixed set of fields representing a product. The server makes new fields optional. The server does two things:

- It ignores optional fields that are empty
- It ignores fields it doesn't know about

This way, the system will function well through change. It doesn't matter which system deploys first. The server exports the new fields only when both the client and server provide them. This is the ideal behavior.

Don't Break Compatibility; Provide a New Endpoint

Here's the punch line. Don't break users of an endpoint, ever. Rather than extending an existing endpoint in incompatible ways, provide a new endpoint to do the new thing. Modern languages have many ways to scope and delegate functions, and these features give us infinite flexibility with naming.

We'll go one step further. Server endpoints are not the only APIs that could stand to benefit from this approach. Everyday function libraries break these rules every day. There's a concept called semantic versioning that says minor versions are compatible, and major versions are possibly incompatible. These rules might look wise, but a far better way is to adopt rules that don't break compatibility in the first place.

It's been a busy chapter, and it's time to wrap up.

Wrap Your Core in a Boundary API

In this chapter, we left our safe bubble of the functional core and ventured out to the real world to deal with state, processes, and communication between components. Here's how we did it.

To begin our exploration, we dove into some techniques to handle composition with inputs and outputs that were less certain. We looked at ways to transform executing errors to data. We also encountered composition using `with`.

Next, we built a server layer in two pieces, the `QuizManager` and the `QuizSession`. We used a `GenServer` to build a quiz and another to let a user take a quiz. The server layer used `start_link` and `handle_call` functions to encapsulate state and handle communication between processes. We eschewed `handle_cast` to handle back pressure issues.

We built validations to make sure our servers will work on consistent data, and then we built an API layer to access our server layer in a convenient way.

It's all starting to come together, but we know our boundary layer supports only one running quiz at a time. In the next chapter, we'll build a dynamic supervisor to allow each user to run a process per quiz. We'll also build a quiz manager to let users build and store multiple quizzes.

You've reached the crux of the book, so turn the page and let's get busy!

CHAPTER 7

Customize Your Lifecycle

In the sentence "Do fun things with big, loud worker-bees" the "L" in "loud" stands for lifecycles. This layer is the part of process machinery that establishes how each component will start, restart, and stop. In this chapter, we'll build and configure the OTP supervisors that form the foundation of our lifecycle control, as shown in the following figure:

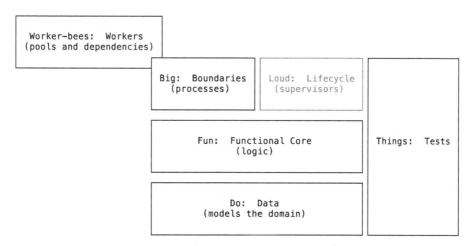

Do fun things with big, loud worker-bees.

The lifecycle layer starts up the OTP server and will take it down, or restart it should the need arise. Components create and destroy each other through their lifecycle layers, and communicate with each other primarily through their boundary APIs.

As we build out the lifecycle layer we'll lean on the OTP supervision architecture. It's going to take us a surprisingly small amount of code, but that code will be dense and require lots of explanation. We will build your intuition as we go, to help you understand what the layers of your project are doing and when. We'll write code soon enough, but first let's take a little bit of time to address a few foundational concepts.

Understand the Lifecycle Building Blocks

We'll risk sounding like a broken record to say your project may never need to create its own processes. Many projects are *libraries*, meaning they'll never need to have their own service layer. They don't need start links or supervisors at all. In the terms we've discussed so far, these libraries will never use the "big, loud worker-bee" layers.

When your project does need processes, it will often use the OTP architecture. OTP might be overkill for some use cases but most often, OTP lets your processes exist seamlessly with others that need the common lifecycle services we'll discuss in the sections that follow. For example, a common OTP architecture means when you start Phoenix, it automatically starts your database pool, if you need it, with a few short lines of configuration.

Let's go one step deeper by defining the different slices of the lifecycle layer and what each one does. We'll start with three main pieces for now: the start link, the supervisor, and the configuration.

The first slice of the lifecycle layer is actually a shared interface that creeps into the boundary. Recall that our boundary layer provided a start_link function (with both /1 and /2 arities) and an init/1 function. Taken together, these functions are part of a *behaviour*, a contract with GenServer. This part of the contract says "Other processes can use these two functions to safely start a process, given an initial value." The function start_link has the _link postfix because the BEAM will notify any process that calls it when the process exits, either normally or abnormally.

You also may have noticed that we don't start the boundary layer directly. That brings us to the second slice of the lifecycle layer, the supervisor. We give that supervisor the job of starting and stopping processes. When any OTP process needs to start another, it must go through the supervisor.

The third slice is the configuration. When any failure happens, the supervisor can follow a procedure to bring it back up again. This procedure is called a *child spec*. Since the BEAM notifies the supervisor any time a linked process fails, the supervisor can use the child spec to determine exactly how to start a new process from scratch, taking other processes into account if necessary.

Let's think about how we might go about tailoring the lifecycle for Mastery. Throughout this chapter, we'll sharpen our understanding of our lifecycle implementation. Generally, these tasks will guide you regardless of your Elixir project:

- Define which types of processes your project needs, and how many of each process

- Appoint a designated process, our supervisor, to start and stop your working processes in an organized repeatable way

- Name and register your processes so supervisors can find and use them at will, even after failure

- Extend this structure hierarchically by defining the child supervisors that we use so one component can manage the lifecycle of many others

Let's peek under the hood at a few of the basic functions Elixir uses to manage processes. In this section, we will look at two of the building blocks that go into OTP: process creation through spawn_link/1 and notification through Process.monitor/1. We won't actually use those functions directly as we build out Mastery, but knowing how they work will help you understand how OTP supervisors work. First, let's start at the beginning, with mix new.

Mix Projects Define Applications

When you type mix new, you're defining a project. At this point, we need to introduce that ambiguous overloaded word we warned you about, *application*. Earlier, we said it's an overloaded and ambiguous term. We told you that we'd use it *only when we have to*. In this section, we're using the term in a specific sense.[1] An application in this sense is *a way to package software* for OTP.

Applications have a specific specification. Here's the one for Mastery. Elixir places the compiled structure inside the _build directory. You can peek inside _build/dev/lib/mastery/ebin/mastery.app:

```
{application,mastery,
            [{applications,[kernel,stdlib,elixir,logger]},
             {description,"mastery"},
             {modules,['Elixir.Mastery','Elixir.Mastery.Application',
                       'Elixir.Mastery.Boundary.QuizManager',
                       'Elixir.Mastery.Boundary.QuizSession',
                       'Elixir.Mastery.Boundary.QuizValidator',
                       'Elixir.Mastery.Boundary.Server',
                       'Elixir.Mastery.Boundary.TemplateValidator',
```

---

1. https://hexdocs.pm/elixir/Application.html

```
      'Elixir.Mastery.Boundary.Validator',
      'Elixir.Mastery.Core.Question',
      'Elixir.Mastery.Core.Quiz',
      'Elixir.Mastery.Core.Response',
      'Elixir.Mastery.Core.Template',
      'Elixir.Mastery.Examples.Math']},
{registered,[]},
{vsn,"0.1.0"}.
```

This is an Erlang file, so the syntax may be a little foreign, but you can still tell what's happening. At the top level, you have a tuple, and the next level down has keyword/value pairs.

Reading the list of tuples from the top, we have the applications Mastery depends on, [kernel,stdlib,elixir,logger]. Next, we have the description, "mastery", and all of the custom modules that we wrote in lib. Next, we have registered, which allows other applications to find this one and vsn, the version number.

If you open up lib/mastery/application.ex, you'll find the code that actually starts our application. Use IO.puts/1 to print a line to the console right after the def start line, like this:

```
defmodule Mastery.Application do
  @moduledoc false

  use Application

  def start(_type, _args) do
    IO.puts "Starting Mastery"
    children = [
    ]
    opts = [strategy: :one_for_one, name: Mastery.Supervisor]
    Supervisor.start_link(children, opts)
  end
end
```

< Now, we'll be able to tell exactly when Mastery formally starts. Most of this file deals with supervisors and child specs. Grossly generalized, supervisors manage lifecycles and child specs configure the lifecycle policies. You don't need to know specifics about those terms yet; we'll address details shortly. What you should understand is that starting our application actually starts our supervisors, and *they* start the processes that make up the application. To prove to ourselves we're in the right place, let's start iex -S mix to fire Application.start:

```
→ iex -S mix
Erlang/OTP 20 [erts-9.0] [source] [64-bit] [smp:12:12] [ds:12:12:10]
[async-threads:10] [hipe] [kernel-poll:false]
```

```
Compiling 1 file (.ex)
Starting Mastery
Interactive Elixir (1.7.4) - press Ctrl+C to exit (type h() ENTER for help)
iex(1)>
```

Voilà. You can see the line we added right after the Compiling 1 file (.ex). Through the course of this chapter, we'll build up application.ex to manage Mastery's lifecycle, adding children to supervise as we go. Before we do so, let's look at the last of the building blocks for supervisors.

Start Processes with Links

Supervisors are built on an interesting primitive: notification. Remember, when a process uses start_link/2 to create a child, the Erlang BEAM will notify the parent process when the child dies. This capability can work in a couple of ways.

First, using spawn_link causes all linked processes to die with the same error if any one of them dies. That may sound like a weird behavior to want, but if the top-level processes of your system die, we don't want their child processes carrying on without them.

Here's how spawn_link works. Let's spawn a process that crashes, like this:

```
iex(1)> spawn fn -> raise "boom" end
#PID<0.86.0>
iex(2)>
10:45:24.797 [error] Process #PID<0.86.0> raised an exception
** (RuntimeError) boom
    (stdlib) erl_eval.erl:668: :erl_eval.do_apply/6
IO.puts "Still alive"
Still alive
:ok
```

In this case, we spawn a process that crashes, and we just keep running as if nothing happened. But if we spawn that process and link it, the behavior is different:

```
iex(1)> spawn_link fn -> raise "boom" end
** (EXIT from #PID<0.84.0>) shell process exited with reason:
    an exception was raised:
    ** (RuntimeError) boom
        (stdlib) erl_eval.erl:668: :erl_eval.do_apply/6

Interactive Elixir (1.7.4) - press Ctrl+C to exit (type h() ENTER for help)
iex(1)>
10:47:36.660 [error] Process #PID<0.86.0> raised an exception
** (RuntimeError) boom
    (stdlib) erl_eval.erl:668: :erl_eval.do_apply/6
```

This second time, we ran linked, and the exception in the spawned process also crashed the IEx shell. You can see that the IEx app's supervisor restarted the shell!

Let's look at a another option, the monitor:

```
iex(1)> {pid, _monitor_ref} = spawn_monitor fn -> raise "boom" end
{#PID<0.109.0>, #Reference<0.1777096488.2680160258.17278>}
iex(2)>
15:26:52.401 [error] Process #PID<0.109.0> raised an exception
** (RuntimeError) boom
    (stdlib) erl_eval.erl:678: :erl_eval.do_apply/6
```

We started a process, this time with a monitor instead of a link. The process we started failed. We don't know it yet, but there's already a message waiting for us. (You might not see the iex(2)> prompt because of the previous failure, but it's there. Just go ahead and type.)

```
flush
{:DOWN, #Reference<0.1777096488.2680160258.17278>, :process, #PID<0.109.0>,
 {%RuntimeError{message: "boom"},
  [{:erl_eval, :do_apply, 6, [file: 'erl_eval.erl', line: 678]}]}}
:ok
```

We flush out all messages, and we can see the :DOWN message. Unlike links, monitors just notify on exit, leaving the process that receives the message to take whatever action is appropriate. Monitors are also one-way, so an exit from the monitoring process doesn't send a message to the monitored process.

Supervisors use a combination of these techniques to manage failures. They link to all processes they start, so those processes will go down if the supervisor goes down. However, they set a special trap_exit flag, so that child processes going down just send messages to the supervisors, similar to how monitors work. A supervisor can then decide which processes to restart, since it wasn't forced to crash.

We won't start and stop GenServer processes with spawn_link or spawn_monitor. Instead, we'll lean on the start_link function to start a process that's linked to a supervisor, so that supervisor process can react to notification of failure.

Now we've seen two of the basic building blocks in action in the context of an application, spawn_link/1 and Process.monitor. Let's put them into action.

Configure Applications to Start Supervisors

Now that we've established some groundwork in vocabulary and you've seen how linked processes work, we should make a plan for what to do with Mastery.

Before we can build out the different supervisors and start links, we need to look at our architecture and think logically about the lifecycles.

We have two kinds of GenServers. We will have exactly one QuizManager server and we'll have one QuizSession server per user. The QuizManager will start when we bring the application up and will remain running throughout.

The QuizSession is a different beast entirely. It's going to have a different lifecycle policy. The supervisor will need to start a QuizSession process when a user takes a quiz and shut it down when they finish a quiz. We will give the processes names so that we can find them easily. Our QuizSession names will be {quiz.title, email} tuples. Those names will be in a specialized registry we'll bring up with the application and keep running throughout. The QuizManager will have a single process named after the module. If a Registry or QuizManager process stops, we'll want it to restart, but if a QuizSession stops, we'll just let it die and let the user start a new one.

Now that we've formed a plan for which servers Mastery will support, we can shift our attention to building out the pieces of the lifecycle layer. Let's start with the QuizManager GenServer.

Create a start_link

The main role of the application will be to provide a packaging structure and lifecycle support for the processes that make up your boundary layer. Here's how it will work.

When your application starts via Application.start, that function doesn't call your boundary's start links directly. Instead, it will call your supervisor's start_link, and that process will start and monitor your application's main processes.

Let's set up our application to start up our QuizManager whenever we start it via mix. That much should be pretty easy to do, since we need only start a single copy of our application. When the supervisor starts, it will call the start_link of the boundary layer. Let's set that up now. Open up quiz_manager.ex and add this start_link callback right below the init callback, like this:

```
Lifecycle/lib/mastery/boundary/quiz_manager.ex
def start_link(options \\ [ ]) do
  GenServer.start_link(__MODULE__, %{ }, options)
end
```

That's all there is to it. We provide the module that defines the GenServer, the initial state of %{}, and options we'll use later, particularly to store the pid by name in a local registry. Recall that we name the QuizManager process with its module name, so we should be able to tell easily if there's one running. Notice when we start IEx, there's no running QuizManager process.

```
iex(1)> alias Mastery.Boundary.QuizManager
Mastery.Boundary.QuizManager
iex(2)> Process.whereis QuizManager
nil
```

The function Process.whereis uses a local process registry to look up the process. As expected, there's no process registered with the QuizManager key. That makes sense because we've not started it yet. We can start one manually using our new start link like this:

```
iex(3)> QuizManager.start_link name: QuizManager
{:ok, #PID<0.133.0>}
iex(4)> pid = Process.whereis QuizManager
#PID<0.133.0>
iex(5)> Process.alive? pid
true
```

Now the process registry has a pid, and the process is alive, and it's bound to the name QuizManager. We're a step closer. The last step in establishing this lifecycle is integrating the work we just did into application.ex.

Configure the Application

The next step is to tell application.ex to automatically use the QuizManager.start_link/3 we just wrote to start a child. In lib/mastery/application.ex, add the following to the list of children, like this:

```
def start(_type, _args) do
  children = [
    { Mastery.Boundary.QuizManager,
      [name: Mastery.Boundary.QuizManager] }
  ]
```

We've told OTP that this application should have a generic supervisor. The following code tells the Supervisor how to get a child specification for this process:

```
{ Mastery.Boundary.QuizManager,
  [name: Mastery.Boundary.QuizManager] }
```

Remember, a child specification defines a supervisor's lifecycle policies, the rules that govern when and how to start and stop a given process.

Our code will call child_spec on the module in the first element of the tuple: Mastery.Boundary.QuizManager. The QuizManager supports that function because use GenServer provides a default implementation. The second element of the tuple is the argument passed in this call, which the default implementation will just forward to our start_link function. That start_link function takes a single argument called options. This will start a QuizManager with the initial state we gave it in the start_link, %{}. The end result is that the supervisor knows how to start a singleton process, stored under the name QuizManager in the process registry, and with the initial value of %{}. That's exactly what we want.

Now shut down IEx, and open it back up. When the application starts, it will start a supervisor. That supervisor will walk down the list of children, starting each one via their start_link functions, using the state in each child spec.

Let's see if it works. We'll walk through a session in IEx, like this:

```
iex(1)> alias Mastery.Boundary.QuizManager
Mastery.Boundary.QuizManager
iex(2)> alias Mastery.Examples.Math
Mastery.Examples.Math
iex(3)> pid = Process.whereis QuizManager
#PID<0.139.0>
iex(4)> Process.alive? pid
true
iex(5)> Supervisor.which_children(Mastery.Supervisor) |> List.last
{Mastery.Boundary.QuizManager, #PID<0.139.0>, :worker,
 [Mastery.Boundary.QuizManager]}
iex(6)> QuizManager.build_quiz Math.quiz_fields
:ok
```

It works! We have a process, it's alive, and it's now supervised. Take a note of the pid, 0.119.0. When you kill the process, the supervisor will start it again:

```
iex(6)> Process.exit pid, :kill
true
iex(7)> pid = Process.whereis QuizManager
#PID<0.127.0>
```

We killed the process using Process.exit. The first attribute is the pid for the process, and the second is the reason code. Then we did a Process.whereis request, and got a pid. Notice the pid of 0.127.0. That's not the same pid we started with! The different pid confirms the restart.

Notice that by building in the start_link and the supervision structure into application.ex, we got both the automatic start of our QuizManager, and failover control. GenServer built the rest in for us by linking the process and trapping exit messages.

Before zooming off to the next topic, let's look at manipulating supervisors in more detail. To explicitly start and stop a supervisor, you'd do this:

```
iex(1)> {:ok, sup_pid} = Supervisor.start_link(
  [%{id: Mastery.Boundary.QuizManager, \
     start: { Mastery.Boundary.QuizManager, :start_link, [[ ]]}}], \
           [strategy: :one_for_one, name: TestSupervisor])
{:ok, #PID<0.144.0>}
iex(2)> Supervisor.stop(TestSupervisor)
:ok
```

Or you can examine the policies our supervisor uses to watch over the Quiz-Manager like this:

```
iex(3)> Mastery.Boundary.QuizManager.child_spec(
  [name: Mastery.Boundary.QuizManager])
%{
  id: Mastery.Boundary.QuizManager,
  start: {Mastery.Boundary.QuizManager, :start_link,
   [[name: Mastery.Boundary.QuizManager]]}
}
```

Child specs are lifecycle policies and you can see one for any GenServer. Now half of Mastery is working so we can shift our focus to the rest, the QuizSession.

Start Per-User Processes with a Dynamic Supervisor

Now we need to start a process per user. Since we don't have a fixed number of processes to start, and since we'll also need to be able to look them up based on a user's attributes, we will need a structure that is a little more sophisticated. We will use a dynamic supervisor.

Most supervisors create processes when an application starts or restarts. That's normally what you want, but not always. A *dynamic supervisor* is a supervisor that starts children dynamically. Since we have no way of knowing who will take quizzes and when, that sounds like exactly what we need. To use a dynamic supervisor, you need many of the same pieces of information:

- You must provide a child spec, the description for how to start and restart processes

- The GenServer you're starting must have a start_link

- You need a strategy for naming and accessing the process

- You must register your dynamic supervisor, perhaps in application.ex

We'll do each of these things in the sections to follow. Let's start at the top, the child spec.

Establish a Child Spec

An OTP child spec is really a policy. It defines how the lifecycle should work for a particular type of process. Remember, lifecycles define behaviors for starts, restarts, and shutdowns.

Our child spec will need to identify the process by name, define exactly how to start the worker process and determine a restart strategy. We'll do those with :id, :start, and :restart keys. Add this child spec to quiz_session.ex, just below the module heading and aliases:

```
Lifecycle/lib/mastery/boundary/quiz_session.ex
def child_spec({quiz, email}) do
  %{
    id: {__MODULE__, {quiz.title, email}},
    start: { __MODULE__, :start_link, [{quiz, email}]},
    restart: :temporary
  }
end
```

This time we manually define a child specification so we can fine-tune it to the needs of managing our named, dynamic processes. Let's go through it key by key.

If you've never worked with child specs before, the :id might not make any sense at all. The :id tuple needs to uniquely identify the process so supervisors can differentiate them.

The :start key has everything OTP needs to invoke our start_link function. It is a tuple with:

- A module
- The name of the function
- And an argument list

Our argument list has one item, the two-tuple {quiz, email}. That's the starting state of our GenServer so we pass it through to the QuizSession.start_link/1 function.

Finally, the :restart key defines the policy for restarts. In our case, if the quiz crashes, we can't really remedy the problem. We'll expect the supervisor to do nothing; we'll just let the user restart. The worst that can happen is that the user may lose mastery scores accumulated along the way. If we wanted to, we could bring in some extra code to store the state and retrieve it in the event of a crash.

Now that we've wired up the start_link, let's establish it in the codebase.

Add a Start Link

Rather than starting our start_link directly, our code is going to use the dynamic supervisor to start the code for us. Let's do that now. Add this code below the child_spec code:

Lifecycle/lib/mastery/boundary/quiz_session.ex
```
def start_link({quiz, email}) do
  GenServer.start_link(
    __MODULE__,
    {quiz, email},
    name: via({quiz.title, email}))
end
```

The start_link itself looks exactly like you'd expect. It specifies the module containing the GenServer, the initial state tuple of {quiz, email}, and the options. We provide a name for the process using a :via tuple, one we'll build with a function. We'll provide this implementation in the listings to follow.

A via tuple is a tuple that OTP uses to register a process. They typically look like {:via, Registry, name}. :via is a fixed atom signalling this technique to OTP. Registry is the module containing the registry we're using, as Elixir has several registry implementations.

The real magic happens in the following take_quiz function you'll add just below start_link:

Lifecycle/lib/mastery/boundary/quiz_session.ex
```
def take_quiz(quiz, email) do
  DynamicSupervisor.start_child(
    Mastery.Supervisor.QuizSession,
    {__MODULE__, {quiz, email}}
  )
end
```

There's the magic. To take a quiz, our code uses the supervisor directly to start a child. We provide the module and the start tuple with our module and initial state. This strategy is at the heart of every OTP application. Don't start processes directly; start them through a supervisor, an intermediary that acts on our behalf to start and monitor our application. As things go wrong, the supervisor can intervene on our behalf.

We still have to touch up the code that will let us name the processes and use them in our code. Let's do that now.

Use Names to Find Services

When you have names in a concurrent system, part of handling failure is referencing your services by name and not pid. That's important because as processes fail, pids change. That means we'll need strategies to find our process IDs by name.

We have a couple of pieces of code to write. We need to implement the function to make our :via tuple and finally plug that function into our API. At the bottom of quiz_session.ex, add this function:

```
Lifecycle/lib/mastery/boundary/quiz_session.ex
  def via({_title, _email}=name) do
    {
      :via,
      Registry,
      {Mastery.Registry.QuizSession, name}
    }
  end
end
```

This builds our :via tuple. Recall the tuple looks like {:via, registry, name}, where registry is the module of the registry implementation and name is a tuple that uniquely identifies the process. In our case, we use the quiz title and user's email.

Now we can start a process and reference it by name. We will need to plug that via lookup into our client API. Let's do that now. Change the API functions to use the via function we wrote previously, like this:

```
Lifecycle/lib/mastery/boundary/quiz_session.ex
def select_question(name) do
  GenServer.call(via(name), :select_question)
end

def answer_question(name, answer) do
  GenServer.call(via(name), {:answer_question, answer})
end
```

Now, each of our API functions calls via(name) to look up the process ID in our registry. Should any process restart, we're protected, and we're also able to access a user's data by quiz title and email as they advance through the quiz. That's all we have to do to quiz_session.ex, so you can save that file.

Add the Registry and Dynamic Supervisor to application.ex

The last step is to plug our registry process and dynamic supervisor into application.ex. Only permanent services get listed here, not transient or temporary processes such as our QuizSession. In other words, we are *making the infrastructure for dynamically creating quizzes* available to our user, and resilient.

Open up application.ex once again and add the children services so that it looks like this:

```
Lifecycle/lib/mastery/application.ex
defmodule Mastery.Application do
  use Application

  def start(_type, _args) do
    children = [
      { Mastery.Boundary.QuizManager,
        [name: Mastery.Boundary.QuizManager] },
      { Registry,
        [name: Mastery.Registry.QuizSession, keys: :unique] },
      { DynamicSupervisor,
        [name: Mastery.Supervisor.QuizSession, strategy: :one_for_one] }
      ]

    opts = [strategy: :one_for_one, name: Mastery.Supervisor]
    Supervisor.start_link(children, opts)
  end
end
```

Each of these tuples is a start specification. It has the module name we're starting and the arguments to pass. The Registry options are :name and :keys. The :name field is the name we'll use for the registry. You've seen that strategy before in our QuizManager. The :keys field allows us to specify whether the keys we register will be unique or not. In our case, they will.

The second tuple is our dynamic supervisor. We don't need to name it but we do need to specify a strategy for restarts. :one_for_one is the right strategy for us. It's a good time to look not just at this strategy, but all of the potential strategies we can establish when we build a child spec.

Establish Supervision Strategies

As you'll recall, when we build a child spec, we define the naming and lifecycle strategies our supervisors will apply to child processes. In general, this configuration code guides OTP in building the lifecycle. Let's talk about what happens when you start a worker.

At startup, the worker will go down the list of child specs and start each of them using the child specs. Some of those child specs will identify other supervisors or applications. Our application.ex child list has both.

Application.start, then, walks down a list of children and starts each one. Those children could be single processes, such as our QuizManager, or they could be applications in their own right. Spinning up a child application means loading that application's child list, and so on. That means our child list is really a *supervison tree.*

Starting your application, then, is pretty straightforward. The children will start in order, and each child will load its own complete supervision tree before the next child starts. Shutting down or restarting the application is another story altogether. You'll need to carefully evaluate dependencies between applications, and specialized shutdown requirements. Here are some questions you might need to consider:

- Do you need to wait for in-progress work to finish?

- After a fixed period of time, should you abandon your attempts to cleanly shutdown?

- Are there dependencies between loading applications?

- Do processes need to load in order?

OTP child specs provide a good amount of detail when it's time to configure the lifecycle policies for a given application. These are the options you have at your disposal as you're making a child spec:

id

   The :id option lets OTP uniquely identify processes managed by supervisors.

start

   The :start tuple has the information the supervisor needs to start a worker, a module, function name, and the argument list with the initial state of the server. There's no strategy here; only the description of a raw function invocation.

restart

   This attribute defines policies for restart. This setting is a strategy. :one_for_one means when a child fails, the supervisor will restart only that child. This strategy makes sense for long-running singletons or pools. :one_for_all means when a child fails, the supervisor will terminate all children and restart all of them. :rest_for_one means when a child fails, the supervisor will terminate and restart all workers started after the failing one. This option makes sense when later processes in the Application.start child list depend on earlier ones.

modules

   This key is primarily managed internally by OTP.

type

:worker or :supervisor. As you know, workers have business logic; supervisors manage lifecycles.

shutdown

This attribute defines the last part of the lifecycle, policies for shutdown. :brutal_kill means immediately, an integer specifies a timeout, and :infinity means wait as long as it takes. Supervisors by default are set to :infinity to let subtrees shut down, but should never be used for workers. Waiting for a process to finish work, pausing for a short period of time to make sure the shutdown happens cleanly, and instantly killing a process are all valid options.

That set of options encapsulates years of experience. This is the strategy that's behind it:

- Repeatable startup is about order.
- Shutdown is about timing.
- Restart is about dependencies.

If you're optimizing startup, all you can hope to do is get the order right. Each supervisor must start its own child list in the order the user specifies. Because supervisors can only start child processes through other supervisors, we're guaranteed an orderly startup that correctly cascades through each of the children.

A working restart then is a combination of the shutdown and startup policies. The user can decide to be as conservative as they want by specifying the three available options. :one_for_one will isolate the restart to a single node; :rest_for_one isolates the supervison tree that started *after* this process; and :one_for_all just brings down all children.

With automation out of the way, let's shift gears to debugging and visualization.

Observe It

We've fully configured the application for Mastery, and we know what those options mean. Think back to the configuration in application.ex. You can probably guess which processes might be running in the application so far:

- A process or two to load the application and start the main Mastery supervisor

- An application supervisor for Mastery

- A quiz manager

- A registry for the QuizSession

- A dynamic supervisor

There may be another housekeeping process or two, but that should be about it. Fortunately, we don't have to guess. We can see exactly what's happening.

Fire up Mastery with iex -S mix, and type :observer.start. We'll open the graphical interface for managing Erlang applications.

When you get there, you'll see a menu near the top of the page that starts with System. The fourth entry or so should be Application. Click it. You'll see a list of applications running on your local computer.

Choose Mastery. You'll see the following process graph. It may not match ours exactly but your graph will be similar to this one:

And it's pretty much what we expected it to be. We see an extra process for a partition for the registry, and a second housekeeping process for the initial application on the far left, but otherwise our guess was exact.

At any time, we can lean on Observer to find out exactly what's going on. We can get memory statistics, message queue length, OTP state and the like. That's going to be especially useful when it's time to debug any OTP application, especially since we've decided to keep a pure functional core. We can get the input values for our functions and we can call our core and find out exactly what will happen.

Now, we have the configuration in application.ex and we've verified that it's working. The next step is to surface our new features in the context of our API. Believe it or not, we've almost completed our full lifecycle support.

Touch Up the API Layer

We've built our boundary layer with an outer API. We know we'll need to make a few changes, but not too many. Here's the bill we have to pay for earlier changes:

- We no longer need to start our QuizManager, so we can remove that API.

- We refer to all QuizSession APIs by pid, and we'll need to change those to use {quiz.title, email} tuples.

- The take_quiz function will shift to our new take_quiz API.

There's not too much work to do. Let's get to it.

The first order of business is to remove the start_quiz_manager API. We no longer need to do that work. Open up mastery.ex and remove the entire function start_quiz_manager. It won't hurt anything, but we may as well be good citizens and keep down our future maintenance requirements. If we need to start a manager at some point in the future, we can use a start_link directly.

Next we need to make select_question and answer_question use {title, email} tuples rather than pids, but wait. Here's the code we have now:

```
def select_question(session) do
  GenServer.call(session, :select_question)
end
```

Here's the code we're going to call:

```
def select_question(name) do ...
```

Here's the lookup function:

```
def via({_title, _email}=name) do ...
```

As long as we're OK with referring to the name tuple as session, that works fine. Realistically, that tuple is naming a session, so we don't need to change any code at all.

The last order of business is to use the take_quiz function in the QuizSession library to establish a new session, like this:

Lifecycle/lib/mastery.ex
```
def take_quiz(title, email) do
  with %Quiz{}=quiz <- QuizManager.lookup_quiz_by_title(title),
       {:ok, _} <- QuizSession.take_quiz(quiz, email)
  do
    {title, email}
  else
    error -> error
  end
end
```

We have inputs, the quiz title, and the email. There's potential failure because the title may not be in the QuizManager. Still, the with statement makes short work of this problem by letting us compose the two functions together, and ignore error conditions until the very end.

Thankfully, that's all we need to do. Let's put the new API to work.

Run with Multiple Users

This trial run will be different from all of the others. We're going to assume our user interface will keep track of the email address for each user, and the quiz they are taking at any given time. Other than that, we'll make no assumptions at all. We'll refer to all processes by some name, and we'll keep track of more than one user at a time.

Let's see how it works:

```
iex(1)> alias Mastery.Examples.Math
Mastery.Examples.Math
iex(2)> email1 = "mathter_of_the_universe@example.com"
"mathter_of_the_universe@example.com"
iex(3)> email2 = "mam_math@example.com"
"mam_math@example.com"
iex(4)> title = Math.quiz.title
:simple_addition
```

We prepare our IEx session with the data we'll need to track a quiz and two users. The next job is to buid a quiz and add the template:

```
iex(5)> Mastery.build_quiz Math.quiz_fields
:ok
iex(6)> Mastery.add_template title, Math.template_fields
:ok
```

Though we've done nothing specifically to start the QuizManager, it's running thanks to the configuration we added in application.ex. Now, we can start individual sessions, like this:

```
iex(7)> user1 = Mastery.take_quiz title, email1
{:simple_addition, "mathter_of_the_universe@example.com"}
iex(8)> user2 = Mastery.take_quiz title, email2
{:simple_addition, "mam_math@example.com"}
iex(9)> Mastery.select_question user1
"5 + 2"
```

Each user took the quiz, establishing a session. We're labeling the session with the {title, email} tuples as expected. We pick a question for the first user.

Let's see what the state looks like internally:

```
iex(10)> :observer.start
:ok
```

Fire up the observer, click on applications and then click on mastery. You'll see the following process diagram, with two running QuizSessions:

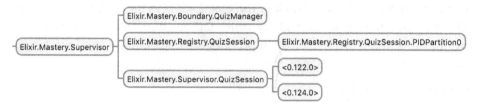

Next, you can actually look at the state of the server. Double click on the top QuizSession process. On our diagram, it's the one labelled 0.122.0, but yours will probably be different:

```
{#{'__struct__' => 'Elixir.Mastery.Core.Quiz',
   current_question =>
       #{'__struct__' => 'Elixir.Mastery.Core.Question',asked => <<"5 + 2">>,
         substitutions => [{...}|...],
         template => #{...}},
   last_response => nil,mastered => [],mastery => 2,record => #{},...},
 <<"mathter_of_the_unive"...>>}
```

You'll be able to see a little Erlang code representing the state, but it should be easy enough for you to read. The question text matches exactly what the user was asked!

Now, you can track both users at the same time. Notice that each must correctly answer two questions in a row:

```
iex(11)> Mastery.answer_question user1, "7"
{"4 + 4", true}
iex(12)> Mastery.select_question user2
"2 + 1"
iex(13)> Mastery.answer_question user1, "8"
:finished
iex(14)> Mastery.answer_question user2, "3"
{"0 + 5", true}
iex(15)> Mastery.answer_question user2, "5"
:finished
```

Excellent! We are tracking two different users, just as we should! We can also tell that the processes are no longer alive. You can check the registry to be sure:

```
iex(16)> Registry.lookup(Mastery.Registry.QuizSession, user1)
[]
```

There's no entry for user1 or user2, and there shouldn't be. We shut down those processes when the user finished. Our lifecycle API is doing exactly what we need it to do so it's a good time to wrap up.

Manage Your Lifecycles with Supervisors

This chapter covered a lot of ground. First, we formed a strategy to incorporate lifecycle management into our application. We planned a single QuizManager and one QuizSession per user. We decided to use a registry to name the processes so that workers could find them as needed.

Next, we built in the requisite start links into our QuizManager and automated the start and supervision in application.ex. We tried it in IEx to verify that it automatically started.

We then built the machinery for dynamic supervision into our QuizSession, including the child spec, the start link and the take_quiz function to invoke the supervisor to create the process. We used the observer to look at our processes in action and even peeked into the state.

Next, we're going to continue our journey by looking at workers. We'll build a persistence layer to save the data for our quiz maker. Then we'll wrap things up by testing the boundary layer and seeing how our components work together.

Keep on plugging. We're almost done. Turn the page!

CHAPTER 8

Summon Your Workers

At last we've come to the "W" in the sentence "Do fun things with big, loud worker-bees." "W" stands for workers. A worker is process machinery that lets us divide labor for reliability, performance, or scalability. The following figure tells the story:

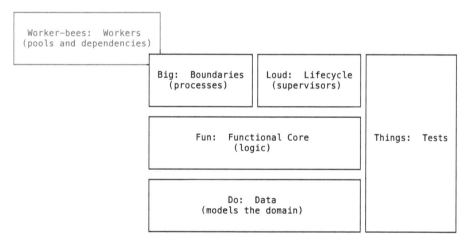

Do fun things with big, loud worker-bees.

Workers are various constructs that provide concurrency. Worker code lives in the boundary with the rest of our process machinery. The worker layer exists to manage concurrency using a variety of tools: naked processes, connection pools, tasks, and other dependencies.

The worker layer is not exactly the lifecycle layer because it lives outside of the OTP policy found in child specs. It is not exactly the boundary layer either because it starts and stops work. It's the worker layer. We separate this layer because often it pays to have a conceptual name for constructs that start and stop work in a concurrent or distributed system.

In this chapter, the first order of business is to look at the concurrency game and help you decide whether to increase your stakes by adding a worker layer. Then we'll look at the ways you might go about summoning and managing workers should you need to do so. We will then solve a problem in Mastery that will require worker machinery, scheduling quizzes. We'll build that feature with another OTP GenServer. Let's get started.

Know Your Motivations

We strongly believe adding concurrency has a price, and it is one that nearly every team will need to pay. Modern developers build distributed, concurrent systems, period. Even the simplest web projects are split into pieces. The web server itself exists to run one user's request concurrently with others. The browser, static content server, and database all use concurrent processes. All but the most basic developers need to deal with concurrency issues presented by those layers, whether or not they decide to introduce their own processes or threads. Knowing how these pieces work will make you a better programmer.

Still, you will want to decide whether to code worker machinery yourself or rely on the work of others to do the job for you. To make that determination, we'll quickly discuss the reasons you might want to introduce workers. We'll focus on three of them: concurrency, isolation, and scalability.

Concurrency

In the simplest terms, concurrency means doing more than one thing at the same time. In our venacular, it's a *micro* concern. A program with a timer requires both a scheduler and an end user's program. A web request firing a long-running task will time out if we don't address the need for concurrency. A client request can farm out six different database requests to six different processes rather than waiting for all of them to return separately, shortening the end user's wait time substantially.

In the core layers, concurrency won't necessarily come into play directly but in the boundary layers where we deal with issues like file I/O and database access, the latency makes concurrency matter more.

Often, Elixir developers will rely on frameworks to implement concurrency concerns for them. For example, if you're working with Phoenix Channels, each connection from each user has its own process. You don't need to lift a finger to do more. Throughout this chapter, we'll look at several different solutions to this problem.

Isolation

Processes aren't just for concurrency. They also insulate users from one another. If the Elixir supervisor only monitored a single system-wide process, it would not be a big deal. In reality, an OTP application is a whole tree of processes so crashes in one user's processes won't impact another.

In the boundary layers, isolation is a big deal. Isolation can limit the damage of failure to a noncritical subsystem. We can build a Twitter integration that won't take our whole system down on failure or we can shut the whole system down if the database layer crashes. In short, developers can make policy decisions based on the needs of the business because we can *isolate one process from another*.

Scaling is the last reason we'll discuss to embrace workers.

Scalability

When you strategically use concurrency across an entire system, Elixir allows a single instance of a program to take advantage of all system cores. In our vernacular, it's a *macro* concern. That capability makes Elixir scale extremely well. Almost always, our strategy for handling scalability will be to pick a good framework that scales well and stay out of the way!

In fact, most of the time in Elixir you're not going to need to introduce your own concurrency abstractions yourself. When we implement workers, we'll be leaning on the work of others, specifically the OTP team. The most important thing is to understand what a framework or tool is doing for you and how to use it appropriately.

We've taken a short peek at *why* we have a worker layer. Now, let's look at *how*. We'll examine some techniques for controlling the processes in your system.

Know Your Tools

You are doubtlessly using Elixir partially because it provides an excellent foundation for concurrency. The worker layer is a concurrency management layer, and in this section, we'll look at the different tools at your disposal to manage concurrency. We will start with some of the most basic ones.

Dependencies will allow us to simply include the work of others. Processes are Elixir concurrency primitives we can certainly lean on in a pinch, but normally we'll be working at a higher level of abstraction. Tasks will allow us to do one-off jobs and still rely on the rich OTP library. Connection pooling libraries let us share long-running connections across processes. Finally, we can integrate into existing frameworks that provide OTP abstractions that serve as containers for our code.

Let's look at the simplest example possible for starting a worker, the dependency.

Leverage Workers in Dependencies

The easiest way to use concurrency in Elixir is to leverage code someone else has already written. When you think about it, that's not such a strange concept. Most of us don't use much recursion in our day to day code because we can lean on Enum's implementations to do that work for us. Many of Elixir's most popular dependencies are full OTP implementations, and most of them take the job of dealing with concurrency off of your plate. For example, when you use Phoenix Channels, you're actually using OTP, and Phoenix deals with the hard parts so you don't have to. The same is true of hundreds of other dependencies. Let's see how that works.

As you saw in Chapter 7, Customize Your Lifecycle, on page 131, each mix project potentially has its own application file, thus its own lifecycle. Unless a dependency specifies app: false, mix will use the policies in the app file to determine how to start, restart or shutdown the application. We can actually see the running dependencies. Let's build an empty app to see what happens:

```
mix new workers
...
iex -S mix
...
```

Now, let's use the Application module to find out what's running, like this:

```
iex(1)> Application.loaded_applications
[
  {:stdlib, 'ERTS  CXC 138 10', '3.7'},
  {:logger, 'logger', '1.8.1'},
  {:kernel, 'ERTS  CXC 138 10', '6.2'},
  {:elixir, 'elixir', '1.8.1'},
  {:compiler, 'ERTS  CXC 138 10', '7.3'},
  {:workers, 'workers', '0.1.0'},
  {:mix, 'mix', '1.8.1'},
  {:iex, 'iex', '1.8.1'}
]
```

That's a surprisingly long list for an empty application, but it makes sense. You may suspect that some of those are due to IEx and mix, but we don't have to guess. Take a look at the worker.app file by typing cat _build/dev/lib/wks/ebin/worker.app, and you'll get this output:

```
{application,worker,
             [{applications,[kernel,stdlib,elixir,logger]},
              {description,"worker"},
              {modules,['Elixir.Worker']},
              {registered,[]},
              {vsn,"0.1.0"}]}.
```

By going down the dependency tree, we can tell exactly which applications Elixir will start, and when. Now, let's add a dependency. Let's add an arbitrary dependency that is an OTP app. Add the dependency { :earmark, "> 1.0.0" } (by the remarkable Dave Thomas) to your application. When you're done, fetch dependencies, like this:

```
mix deps.get
...
iex -S mix
...
```

Now let's look at the application dependencies again, and the list will be longer:

```
iex(1)> Application.loaded_applications
[
  {:stdlib, 'ERTS  CXC 138 10', '3.7'},
  {:logger, 'logger', '1.8.1'},
  {:earmark,
   'Earmark is a pure-Elixir Markdown converter..., '1.3.2'},

  ...
]
```

We didn't even have to add the dependencies to application.ex! In other words, OTP applications are the default type of dependency. If we had a dependency that was a library without its own .app file, we'd specify the dependency with the flag app: false flag in mix.exs. Earmark is an OTP dependency with an .app file, so that means when we use Earmark, starting our own application starts Earmark as well. You can even verify that's true by looking at the new applications tuple in the worker.app file:

```
{application,workers,
             [{applications,[kernel,stdlib,elixir,logger,earmark]},
              {description,"workers"},
...
```

And when we take advantage of the features of Earmark, it will have its own OTP lifecycle as a child of our server, and we'll be able to take advantage of them by merely using the Earmark API.

With the simplest way to spin up workers, let's look at the most primitive, naked Elixir processes and why we might want to avoid them in favor of higher abstractions.

Generally, Avoid Naked Processes

The natural go-to concurrency construct for Elixir beginners is the process, but we strongly believe that instead, you will normally want to incorporate proven features that have already addressed the subtle complexities of concurrency. Still, we'll cover processes here so you can put them in context when the inevitable edge cases do occur.

We've already spent a bit of time using Elixir primitives for processes, but it bears repeating. We have access to the primitives to send messages with send/2, spawn processes with the various versions of spawn/n, and spawn_monitor/n. Typically, we will want our processes to be OTP processes because we'll want to take advantage of the GenServer lifecycle. Elixir can't manage what it doesn't know about.

You'll rarely send messages with the send varients, though you might use some of its close cousins. Process.send_after and :timer.send_interval are useful for dealing with various scheduling problems, but those are exceptions. The rule of thumb is to use higher abstractions to work with processes, so let's move up the food chain to a pretty simple alternative to naked processes, the task.

Make Serial Code Concurrent with Tasks

Elixir has a nice abstraction for executing one-time single-purpose jobs in a process, the task. Generally, you'll fire a task, go do some work and then await the results. Tasks are great for making sequential code concurrent. Let's look at a couple of different ways to handle long-running jobs.

An easy way to run two slow jobs concurrently is to use Task.async/1 and Task.await/1, like this:

```
task = Task.async(fn -> Slow.job1() end)
slow_job2()
Task.await(task)
```

That code fires the first slow job and runs it in a separate process. While that's processing, it fires the second job, and finally awaits the results of the first job. It doesn't really matter which job finishes first; either the first job will finish early and will wait, or the second process will finish early and the first won't have to wait. The code will be much faster on average if the jobs take roughly the same amount of time.

You might be tempted to generalize this approach, like this:

```
def multi_task(slow_funs) do
  slow_funs
  |> Enum.map(&Task.async/1)
  |> Enum.map(&Task.await/1)
end
```

That code will work OK until you start throwing real numbers at it. Then, you'll be in trouble. Let's say you're using that code to smooth out some very slow database transactions. You'll increase the proportion of long transactions until you swamp your database pool by creating too many requests to process at once. In short, we've removed backpressure for our worst database calls!

What you really need is a way to spread that work out. Even better, you would like to divide the work optimally, *based on the number of cores supported by your hardware*. And that's precisely what Task.async_stream/2 does for you:

```
def multi_task(slow_funs) do
  slow_funs
  |> Task.async_stream(fn(f) -> f.() end)
  |> Enum.map(fn {:ok, x} -> x end)
end
```

This code is a little tricky, but it's worth understanding. Task.async_stream/3 takes three arguments:

- A list of items
- A function to call in a task
- The maximum number of tasks to run at a time

We pass a list of functions into the first argument. These functions identify slow work. Then, we define a simple little function that takes a function and invokes it. The result is that the first list of functions will be called in a task.

Here's the good part. The last argument defaults to System.schedulers_online/0., and that's usually the number of cores! We get all the concurrency we can use but not more.

We can easily do some work like this:

```
[users, projects] =
  [&fetch_users(user_filter), &fetch_projects(project_filter)]
  |> multi_task
```

Marvelous! It's now trivial to take two high-latency jobs and do them at the same time. In a sense, we have built a narrow type of pool, one to share processes. Erlang also has a great general-purpose solution for pooling resources called Poolboy.

Build Pools of Common Resources with Poolboy

Poolboy is an Erlang application for sharing pools of common resources. Sometimes programs need to use processes that take a while to start. In such instances, it's best to have a pool of processes to share across a whole project. It's ideal for situations where you need to throttle many requests down to a smaller number of resources. For example, most web servers run thousands of concurrent jobs through a handful of database connections because those connections often consume a good amount of memory and take a while to start.

Since Poolboy is an OTP application, you already know how to use it. Just add a dependency, configure it in application.ex, and create an OTP server to do some work.

In the configuration in application.ex, you can specify the number of permanent and temporary workers, like this:

```
defmodule MyApp.Application do
  @moduledoc false

  use Application

  defp poolboy_config do
    [
      {:name, :worker_pool},
      {:worker_module, MyApp.Worker},
      {:size, 3},
      {:max_overflow, 2}
    ]
  end

  def start(_type, _args) do
    children = [
      :poolboy.child_spec(:worker, poolboy_config())
    ]

    opts = [strategy: :one_for_one, name: PoolboyApp.Supervisor]
    Supervisor.start_link(children, opts)
  end
end
```

You've seen this code before. This configuration for a mix project called MyApp would have three permanent workers and two additional workers that go away once they complete their work.

A worker is a pure OTP GenServer, and works something like this:

```
defmodule MyApp.Worker do
  use GenServer

  def start_link(_) do
    GenServer.start_link(__MODULE__, nil, [])
  end

  def init(_) do
    {:ok, nil}
  end

  def handle_call({:process_work, x}, _from, state) do
    IO.puts("Doing work for #{inspect(self())} #{x}")
    # do work here
    {:reply, result, state}
  end
end
```

We have functions to start the server process and an empty init. Then we have the typical handle_call that does whatever work you want it to do in the commented area. All in all, this code is just a bare OTP server, one where the state doesn't really matter. Invoking a worker looks like this:

```
:poolboy.transaction(
  :worker_pool,
  fn(pid) ->
    GenServer.call(pid, request)
  end)
```

We make a direct call to the Erlang module :poolboy, wrapping the GenServer.call/2 in a function. That's all there is to it.

This Poolboy example is a great illustration of leveraging other frameworks to provide workers. We don't need to know the details underneath. We just configure our policies and let the chosen framework do the work.

In the next section, we're going to implement a scheduling solution. We'll rely on OTP plus simple message passing to schedule timed tests that will stop quizzes at a scheduled time. Let's look at how that will work.

Add a Proctor to Run Timed Quizzes

To be useful in a classroom setting, Mastery should be able to schedule quizzes. Step by step, here's the flow for the major actors working with Mastery:

1. A teacher schedules a quiz.

2. At the quiz's scheduled starting time, the proctor makes that quiz available in the quiz manager.

3. A student takes a quiz.

4. At the scheduled end time, the proctor automatically stops all student processes for that quiz and removes the quiz from the manager.

This is exactly the kind of machinery that defines the worker layer. It's not lifecycle code because it lives outside of the configured lifecycle policies in our GenServers. It goes beyond simple boundary code because it will stop GenServer processes. This is the domain of the worker layer.

We'll implement it with a GenServer and a boundary API. Let's look at scheduling a quiz first. We'll write an API function in Mastery, one that will call the API function in our as-yet unwritten Boundary GenServer module.

Establish the Boundary API

Let's work from the outside in. Sometimes, working in this direction gives us an idea of what our API will look like before we dive into the details. The boundary layer will need a complex API to schedule a quiz so it will be available to users. We will start with the usual aliases:

```
Workers/lib/mastery.ex
defmodule Mastery do
  alias Mastery.Boundary.{QuizSession, QuizManager, Proctor}
  alias Mastery.Boundary.{TemplateValidator, QuizValidator}
  alias Mastery.Core.Quiz
```

We add a simple alias for Proctor. Note that this code looks like our other boundary functions, and this organization is not unusual. The worker layer does not change the way we organize our *code* from what we normally do on the boundary. Rather, the worker layer will define the way we organize *processes* outside of the typical policies in the lifecycle layer.

Let's provide the API function from Mastery:

Workers/lib/mastery.ex
```
def schedule_quiz(quiz, templates, start_at, end_at) do
  with :ok <- QuizValidator.errors(quiz),
       true <- Enum.all?(templates, &(:ok == TemplateValidator.errors(&1))),
       :ok <- Proctor.schedule_quiz(quiz, templates, start_at, end_at),
  do: :ok, else: (error -> error)
end
```

Scheduling a quiz should take the typical quiz and template fields. We also need a couple of DateTime timestamps for the beginning and ending of the test session.

Now, we can move onto the boundary. We will start with the Proctor boundary layer.

Write the Proctor Boundary Server

We'll create a new Proctor module in the Boundary namespace to implement a GenServer to schedule quizzes. It's a single API, Proctor.schedule_quiz, but a complex one. Let's walk through it step by step.

Create a new file lib/mastery/boundary/proctor.ex so we can establish our GenServer:

Workers/lib/mastery/boundary/proctor.ex
```
defmodule Mastery.Boundary.Proctor do
  use GenServer
  require Logger
  alias Mastery.Boundary.{QuizManager, QuizSession}
```

We create the usual ceremonial module definition and a few aliases. We'll need access to both managers and the logger, but nothing else.

Next, we initialize the server and create a start link, like this:

Workers/lib/mastery/boundary/proctor.ex
```
def start_link(options \\ [ ]) do
  GenServer.start_link(__MODULE__, [ ], options)
end

def init(quizzes) do
  {:ok, quizzes}
end
```

We need only one Proctor GenServer, so the start_link is trivial. We simply name the GenServer a module. We initialize with a list of quizzes.

Next, we will write the GenServer code to schedule a quiz. Once again, we'll work from the outside in, starting with our API.

```
Workers/lib/mastery/boundary/proctor.ex
def schedule_quiz(proctor \\ __MODULE__, quiz, temps, start_at, end_at) do
  quiz = %{
    fields: quiz,
    templates: temps,
    start_at: start_at,
    end_at: end_at
  }
  GenServer.call(proctor, {:schedule_quiz, quiz})
end
```

That's simple enough. We create a quiz and pass it straight through to the GenServer with a handle_call. Now, we dive into the gritty details. Don't let anyone tell you differently. Concurrent systems are complex, and it's the interactions between processes that make them so. Still, our end users need to schedule quizzes as a foundational capibility for Mastery so we will move forward to the heart of our scheduler.

Let's look at that outer handle_call for :schedule_quiz, where things start to get a little more interesting.

This service will add the quiz to be scheduled, order the quizzes in the scheduler to make them easier to deal with, start any quizzes that need to be managed, and then build a reply tuple, like this:

```
Workers/lib/mastery/boundary/proctor.ex
def handle_call({:schedule_quiz, quiz}, _from, quizzes) do
  now = DateTime.utc_now
  ordered_quizzes =
    [quiz | quizzes]
    |> start_quizzes(now)
    |> Enum.sort(fn a, b ->
      date_time_less_than_or_equal?(a.start_at, b.start_at)
    end)
  build_reply_with_timeout({:reply, :ok}, ordered_quizzes, now)
end
```

We calculate the current time, and then build a list of all of the quizzes from the new inbound quiz and the current GenServer state. We pipe that list to a function to start all of the quizzes that need starting, and then sort the remaining quizzes.

Let's talk about the reply. It needs to set the state of the GenServer and also set a timeout, so we'll get control back for starting the next quiz. In this code, we're going to make use of a little-used GenServer feature, appending an optional timeout to a :reply tuple. When we're done, our :reply tuple should look like {:reply, :ok, quizzes, timeout}. The timeout is optional, so if the quizzes are empty, we'll leave it off.

Our code, then, returns any quizzes that have not yet been started, and tacks on a timeout so that we'll get control back in time to start the next quiz.

Whew! With the broad strokes coded, let's see how we go about building that reply tuple:

```
Workers/lib/mastery/boundary/proctor.ex
defp build_reply_with_timeout(reply, quizzes, now) do
  reply
  |> append_state(quizzes)
  |> maybe_append_timeout(quizzes, now)
end

defp append_state(tuple, quizzes), do: Tuple.append(tuple, quizzes)

defp maybe_append_timeout(tuple, [], _now), do: tuple
defp maybe_append_timeout(tuple, quizzes, now) do
  timeout =
    quizzes
    |> hd
    |> Map.fetch!(:start_at)
    |> DateTime.diff(now, :millisecond)

  Tuple.append(tuple, timeout)
end
```

Remember, handle_call and handle_info take two different kinds of responses and our function will need to support one of each. Therefore, we call the function with a base tuple, say {:reply, :ok} for a handle_call. We then append the quizzes and optionally append a timeout.

To append the quizzes, we have a tiny one-line function that just delegates to Tuple.append/2. You might be wondering why we didn't just pipe to Tuple.append/2. The reason is that we want to name the concept for future readers of this code. It's easy to understand a flow of starting with a tuple, appending the GenServer state and then appending a timeout. We're just maintaining a uniform level of abstraction.

The last function picks off the head of the list and calculates the date math based on now and quiz.start. These three functions represent the heart of our scheduler. Don't move on until you understand them!

There are plenty more details to handle. Next, let's look at how we'll start quizzes when timeouts do occur:

```
Workers/lib/mastery/boundary/proctor.ex
defp start_quizzes(quizzes, now) do
  {ready, not_ready} = Enum.split_while(quizzes, fn quiz ->
    date_time_less_than_or_equal?(quiz.start_at, now)
  end )
  Enum.each(ready, fn quiz -> start_quiz(quiz, now) end)
  not_ready
end
```

Next, we shift from the ceremony of scheduling quizzes to the work of actually starting them. We split the remaining quizzes into two groups, those that are ready to be scheduled and those that aren't. For each one of the ready ones, we call start_quiz. We return the quizzes that have not yet been scheduled.

Since we're working with DateTime, we write a quick function to shape our inputs so that we can use Elixir's library to process the date difference so we don't have to write the date/time comparison ourselves.

Now, let's look at what happens when we start an individual quiz:

```
Workers/lib/mastery/boundary/proctor.ex
def start_quiz(quiz, now) do
  Logger.info "Starting quiz #{quiz.fields.title}..."
  QuizManager.build_quiz(quiz.fields)
  Enum.each(quiz.templates, &add_template(quiz, &1))
  timeout = DateTime.diff(quiz.end_at, now, :millisecond)
  Process.send_after(self(), {:end_quiz, quiz.fields.title}, timeout)
end

defp date_time_less_than_or_equal?(a, b) do
  DateTime.compare(a, b) in ~w[lt eq]a
end
```

We're getting close to the finish line. We build the quiz, add each template and then add the result to the QuizManager. Then, we use Process.send_after to send a message to end the quiz when it's done.

Now we have to process that timeout we set when we were scheduling a quiz:

```
Workers/lib/mastery/boundary/proctor.ex
def handle_info(:timeout, quizzes) do
  now = DateTime.utc_now
  remaining_quizzes = start_quizzes(quizzes, now)
  build_reply_with_timeout({:noreply}, remaining_quizzes, now)
end
```

GenServer timeouts are one of the most underused features in OTP. Loosely stated, a timeout says "If nothing is happening in x milliseconds, I'll make it happen." More specifically, if no message is received before the timeout occurs, OTP will send the scheduled timeout. That's ideal for our purposes.

We process a handle_info where we basically take advantage of two functions we've already built, start_quizzes and build_reply_with_timeout.

Last of all, we need to stop a quiz at it's end time. We've already sent the timeout so all that remains is for us to process it:

Workers/lib/mastery/boundary/proctor.ex
```
  def handle_info({:end_quiz, title}, quizzes) do
    QuizManager.remove_quiz(title)
    title
    |> QuizSession.active_sessions_for
    |> QuizSession.end_sessions
    Logger.info "Stopped quiz #{title}."
    handle_info(:timeout, quizzes)
  end
end
```

We remove the quiz from the quiz manager and then lean on unwritten functions in QuizSession to get a list of titles and end all running quizzes with that title. Then, we return the state to the GenServer, unchanged.

With the Proctor coded, we can move on to the remaining integrations in QuizSession and QuizManager.

Integrate the Proctor into the Boundary

Our Proctor is a masterpiece, but we still have to wire it in to the rest of Mastery. The boundary has two different points of integration. We will need to revise the QuizManager to return the active sessions for a quiz and also adapt QuizSession to end the sessions for a given title as our scheduler terminates them. Those integrations should go quickly.

A big part of the battle of building concurrent systems is finding the processes so we can manage them. That's the domain of the registry. To get the existing sessions with a given title, we're going to lean on our supervisor and the corresponding registry for our dynamic supervisor. Open up lib/mastery/boundary/quiz_session.ex and add this function to return active sessions:

Workers/lib/mastery/boundary/quiz_session.ex
```
def active_sessions_for(quiz_title) do
  Mastery.Supervisor.QuizSession
  |> DynamicSupervisor.which_children
  |> Enum.filter(&child_pid?/1)
  |> Enum.flat_map(&active_sessions(&1, quiz_title))
end
```

We start with the name for our supervisor, Mastery.Supervisor.QuizSession. This is the one we configured in application.ex. We can use that key to find the processes registered by our supervisor. We pipe that to DynamicSupervisor.which_children/1 and filter those registry entries to a a custom function to pick off pids which should give us active processes. From those, we flat map across another custom function that lets us accumulate active sessions.

Let's build those two helper functions, one to filter registry entries and one to determine which ones are active:

```
Workers/lib/mastery/boundary/quiz_session.ex
defp child_pid?({:undefined, pid, :worker, [__MODULE__]})
when is_pid(pid) do
  true
end
defp child_pid?(_child), do: false

defp active_sessions({:undefined, pid, :worker, [__MODULE__]}, title) do
  Mastery.Registry.QuizSession
  |> Registry.keys(pid)
  |> Enum.filter(fn {quiz_title, _email} ->
    quiz_title == title
  end)
end
```

child_pid? is a two-headed function that takes a registry tuple and filters out the active processes. Our function takes in registry keys and identifies entries for our module that match the pid we're seeking. If the first head matches, we'll return true; otherwise, we'll return false. When we're through this filter, we have a list of the registry entries for active quizzes.

The active_sessions function works by finding all of the keys associated with each pid. Those keys are the {email, quiz_title} tuples we establish for each session. We look up all of those sessions that match the titles we're looking for so we can take action.

Of course, the action we want to take is to be unkind to those processes by shutting them down. Add this last bit to end the sessions:

```
Workers/lib/mastery/boundary/quiz_session.ex
def end_sessions(names) do
  Enum.each(names, fn name -> GenServer.stop(via(name)) end)
end
```

We can take the registry tuples and stop the session, using the via(name) function for each tuple. That's all that needs to happen to the session manager, but we still need to do a little integration to our quiz manager.

In the boundary manager, we need only to remove quizzes once the proctor is through with them. That's pretty trivial. First, add this API to lib/mastery/boundary/quiz_manager.ex, like this:

Workers/lib/mastery/boundary/quiz_manager.ex
```
def remove_quiz(manager \\ __MODULE__, quiz_title) do
    GenServer.call(manager, {:remove_quiz, quiz_title})
  end
```

That simple function is just a GenServer.call, passing in the title of the quiz. The server implementation is almost as small:

Workers/lib/mastery/boundary/quiz_manager.ex
```
def handle_call({:remove_quiz, quiz_title}, _from, quizzes) do
  new_quizzes = Map.delete(quizzes, quiz_title)
  {:reply, :ok, new_quizzes}
end
```

It's a simple Map.delete, and we return the new state to the GenServer. Now, we add our dependencies to application.ex, like this:

Workers/lib/mastery/application.ex
```
children = [
  { Mastery.Boundary.QuizManager,
    [name: Mastery.Boundary.QuizManager] },
  { Registry,
    [name: Mastery.Registry.QuizSession, keys: :unique] },
  { Mastery.Boundary.Proctor,
    [name: Mastery.Boundary.Proctor] },
  { DynamicSupervisor,
    [name: Mastery.Supervisor.QuizSession, strategy: :one_for_one] }
  ]
```

And we're done! Take a breath. We're finally at the point where we can try it out.

Put the Proctor to Work

That's a lot of code without anything to show for it, but we finally get to sample the wares. Here's a taste for what it can do. First, let's schedule a quiz:

```
iex(1)> alias Mastery.Examples.Math
Mastery.Examples.Math
iex(2)> alias Mastery.Boundary.QuizSession
Mastery.Boundary.QuizSession
iex(3)>
nil
iex(4)> now = DateTime.utc_now()
#DateTime<2019-05-09 13:33:22.337162Z>
iex(5)> five_seconds_from_now = DateTime.add(now, 5)
```

```
#DateTime<2019-05-09 13:33:27.337162Z>
iex(6)> one_minute_from_now = DateTime.add(now, 60)
#DateTime<2019-05-09 13:34:22.337162Z>
iex(7)> Mastery.schedule_quiz(Mastery.Examples.Math.quiz_fields(),
...(7)> [Math.template_fields()], five_seconds_from_now, one_minute_from_now)
:ok
iex(8)>
```

Now we have a quiz scheduled. Wait a few seconds and it will come online:

```
08:33:27.337 [info]  Starting quiz simple_addition...
```

It's online! Remember, you might not get an IEx prompt, but it's there. We can take the quiz like this:

```
Mastery.take_quiz(Math.quiz_fields().title, "james@graysoftinc.com")
{:simple_addition, "james@graysoftinc.com"}
iex(9)> QuizSession.active_sessions_for(
...(9)>   Mastery.Examples.Math.quiz_fields().title)
[simple_addition: "james@graysoftinc.com"]
```

We can see the quiz in active session! Now wait a minute or so and we'll get notice that it's been terminated:

```
iex(12)>
08:34:22.353 [info]  Stopped quiz simple_addition.
nil
```

As expected, we get the message. Press Enter if you like to get a new prompt. Then we'll try to list active sessions again:

```
iex(12)>
08:34:22.353 [info]  Stopped quiz simple_addition.
nil
iex(13)> QuizSession.active_sessions_for(Math.quiz_fields().title)
[]
```

And there are no longer active sessions!

This is a distributed system, and as with all of them, there are trade-offs. We need to establish a policy. If our server crashes midstream, we'll lose the timeouts that have already been set. Maybe this is OK; a crash could just notify the proctor and they could intervene manually.

But maybe we want to do a little bit of extra work to rehydrate the data in the event of a crash but the init callback gives us a perfectly convenient place to add that code. If you decide that's where Mastery should go, we'll leave that code for you to write!

We've covered a lot of ground, so it's a good time to wrap up.

Summon Your Workers

This chapter presented the worker layer, the process machinery that manages concurrency apart from lifecycle policy. We framed the discussion in three parts: the reasons to adopt a worker layer, the tools we might use for doing so, and the implementation of worker concepts to build a scheduler.

First, we established three primary motivations for introducing a worker layer: concurrency, isolation and scalability. Concurrency is a focused issue that allows more than one task to happen at a time, often reducing latency or enabling a feature like a scheduler. Isolation improves system reliability by limiting the damage any single bug can do by crashing a process. Scalability is a broader architectural concern, allowing one program to run across many processes.

We moved on to some of the tools for implementing a worker layer. By far the preferred approach we introduced was to leverage other dependencies to do work for us. The GenServer application architecture allows us to mix in Elixir or Erlang dependencies such as Poolboy that spin up their own applications with their own worker layers that we can leverage through an API. Tasks also allow single-purpose one-shot functions to fire concurrently with our application code.

Finally, we put these ideas into practice with our own worker layer. We relied on GenServer's timeouts to implement a schedule, and we used various GenServer and Registry APIs to start, find and stop Mastery processes.

We've made it through all of the layers in our sentence, "Do fun things with big, loud worker-bees" but there's still work to do. In the next chapter, we'll integrate persistence with an external dependency. We'll also explore how our strategy plays with librares such as Phoenix LiveView and Scenic. When you're ready, turn the page and we'll see how our components work together!

CHAPTER 9

Assemble Your Components

Congratulations on making it through all of the layers in a single OTP project, from data to workers. In this chapter, we're going to focus on putting these layers into context. We'll help you answer the core question: how do our projects work with others, whether they are external dependencies or projects we build? This overarching question has two undergirding concerns.

The first concern is how components interact with *dependencies*, particularly in more complex interfaces. The questions this concern opens up are serious: How might we implement persistence? How do our layers relate to user interfaces? Generally, how do our components connect to the rest of the world without coupling too tightly?

Consider persistence. If we rush into designing a new project by going straight to a database schema and wiring that schema directly to database functions, we'll be running to the boundary layer before building a core. We'll miss an opportunity to explore a true functional core free from boundary concerns of heavy side effects and process machinery. For example, business problems often demand state machines, and those types of projects benefit tremendously from delaying the persistence implementation until the transitions of the state machine are fully settled.

The second concern is how components fit into existing *frameworks*. The questions in this area are weighty: Do worker-bees play nicely with emerging frameworks like LiveView or Scenic? How do these components play with Phoenix Channels? With those questions in mind, let's seek some answers.

Add Persistence as a Boundary Service

In most Elixir projects, we inevitably begin our data layer with schemas and go from there. We tack on queries and services that use them to count, save, and summarize things. Ecto makes that much easy. What emerges might be a unified API, but it will be one that *combines the issues of boundary and core*. We, the authors know. We're guilty of the same thing. The problem is that when we build software like this, we take on too much at once. Our software doesn't get the benefits of the separation of concerns, and each reader of the code is doomed to deal with too much complexity at once.

This approach is *not* a functional one. In fact, we're making a number of commitments, often from the first few hours of developments:

- Our database schemas will have the same shape as our projects.
- Our core code will be *thin* and our boundary code will be *thick*.
- Often, we won't have a separate core layer, at all!

Sometimes, this early database coupling doesn't work against us. In some cases, a struct exists purely as a conduit in a tightly coupled flow that passes straight from an API and directly into a database. Think audit records.

Other times, it pays to *think*. For example, building Mastery without considering Ecto integration at all led us to an interesting design, one where the foundational Quiz design allows us to advance from question to question based on correct answers without the benefit of a database at all.

It turns out that the main things we might want to persist are quiz designs and responses. In this section, we'll focus on persisting responses. Our persistence solution will allow us to save responses as a user takes a quiz. Then, admins can review reports of the responses to quizzes.

As with most database integrations, we'll take advantage of a framework to manage our concurrency for us: Ecto, the most popular persistence framework for Elixir.

Manage Persistence with Callbacks

Let's build our persistence solution. Fair warning. We're going to write a bit more code to start with, including a second Response model. We think the benefits will be worth it. The second response will not be exactly the same as the first, because *each response struct solves a different problem*. One captures user responses and the other persists them to the database.

We'll manage persistence with callbacks, tweaking Mastery to take a function we'll call when each new response is submitted. In some solutions, perhaps with an online practice quiz, if we don't need to save responses, that function will do nothing. In others, that function will save responses to the database.

We're not suggesting that every project be built this way. In fact, this persistence strategy may be dead wrong if you're worried about moving too much data, or your solution is too distributed, or if your solution risks integrity problems.

We're suggesting that you *think*. Database coupling can be absolutely toxic. Developers should strongly consider reducing the coupling between the database layer and the rest of your project. Furthermore, it's often a good idea to imagine how you'll go about isolating a pure functional core.

Build a Poncho Project

We've determined that we want to use Mastery in a couple of use cases, some which require permanent persistence to a database and some that don't. For such a situation, we'll want to be able to create a persistence solution as a dependency.

A convenient way to do so is through a poncho project. It's not a term that we invented, but it's an almost trivial concept. We'll just create the dependency from within the mastery directory, but its code will live outside lib and have its own lib directory. The advantage to this approach is that we'll be able to grow these two projects within the same codebase and still reduce coupling. When it's time to separate them at the directory level we'll be able to tweak the mix dependencies, check them into different repositories and everything else will *just work*.

You can accomplish similar goals with umbrellas, a mix construct that lets you manage multiple applications with tighter coupling but less ceremony. Use the solution that feels right for you. We're going to blow through the ceremony of creating a new Ecto project quickly because that information can be found elsewhere. Still, in the interest of completeness, we feel obligated to list all of the steps, so let's go.

From the mastery directory, create the project:

```
mix new mastery_persistence --sup
```

We created a full mix project with a full application.ex file that defines our supervision structure. Notice the application entry in mix.exs:

```
Persistence/mastery_persistence/mix.exs
def application do
  [
    extra_applications: [:logger],
    mod: {MasteryPersistence.Application, []}
  ]
end
```

And add the Ecto dependencies to mix.exs:

Persistence/mastery_persistence/mix.exs
```
defp deps do
  [
    {:ecto_sql, "~> 3.1"},
    {:postgrex, "~> 0.14.1"}
  ]
end
```

The only dependencies we need are ecto_sql and postgrex, so we add them. Make sure to fetch dependencies:

```
→ mix deps.get
Resolving Hex dependencies...
New:
...
→
```

Dependencies fetched! Now change config/config.exs to add the Ecto repo:

Persistence/mastery_persistence/config/config.exs
```
use Mix.Config

config :mastery_persistence,
  ecto_repos: [MasteryPersistence.Repo]

config :logger, level: :info

import_config "#{Mix.env()}.exs"
```

We added the MasteryPersistence.Repo so we are ready to change dev.exs and test.exs to configure the Postgres connections, like this:

Persistence/mastery_persistence/config/dev.exs
```
use Mix.Config

config :mastery_persistence, MasteryPersistence.Repo,
  database: "mastery_dev",
  hostname: "localhost"
```

With persistence configured for dev.exs, we can move on to test.exs:

Persistence/mastery_persistence/config/test.exs
```
use Mix.Config

config :mastery_persistence, MasteryPersistence.Repo,
  database: "mastery_test",
  hostname: "localhost",
  pool: Ecto.Adapters.SQL.Sandbox
```

Our dev.exs and test.exs configurations point to separate databases as they should and our Test configuration points to the Ecto.Adapters.SQL.Sandbox pool which has some tools to speed up our tests.

Now, we can finally write some code! Our first stop: the Repo and Response modules.

Persist the Responses

We've done some tedious work to prepare our project to work with Ecto. Now we need to deal with concurrency. As you saw in Chapter 7, Customize Your Lifecycle, on page 131, the nice thing is that we can deal with lifecycle concerns with policy configuration and not code.

Open up lib/mastery_persistence/application.exs and add these lines:

```
children = [
  MasteryPersistence.Repo
]
```

The Repo has the Ecto processes that will access our database. With this configuration, we're giving OTP the responsibility of starting them up and shutting them down cleanly. Let's build that repo now, like this:

Persistence/mastery_persistence/lib/mastery_persistence/repo.ex
```
defmodule MasteryPersistence.Repo do
  use Ecto.Repo,
    otp_app: :mastery_persistence,
    adapter: Ecto.Adapters.Postgres
end
```

It's dead simple; we call use Ecto.Repo to mix in the code we'll need, taking all of the defaults.

With the usual ceremony for setting up the project for Ecto out of the way, we can address the schema. In Ecto, the schema connects the Elixir struct to the database schema.

In Mastery, we will save only the responses. Add the file lib/mastery_persistence/response.ex:

Persistence/mastery_persistence/lib/mastery_persistence/response.ex
```
defmodule MasteryPersistence.Response do
  use Ecto.Schema
  import Ecto.Changeset

  @mastery_fields ~w[quiz_title template_name to email answer correct]a
  @timestamps ~w[inserted_at updated_at]a
```

We define the module and include the usual Ecto ceremony. Also we define the @mastery_fields and @timestamps to save us a little typing later on. Now, we can create the fields for our schema. There are no surprises:

Persistence/mastery_persistence/lib/mastery_persistence/response.ex

```
schema "responses" do
  field :quiz_title, :string
  field :template_name, :string
  field :to, :string
  field :email, :string
  field :answer, :string
  field :correct, :boolean

  timestamps()
end
```

That's a typical Ecto schema, with the fields from our Mastery response plus a silent id field and a couple of timestamps. There's just one function we need, the one that actually builds the changeset we'll use to persist the struct:

Persistence/mastery_persistence/lib/mastery_persistence/response.ex

```
  def record_changeset(fields) do
    %__MODULE__{ }
    |> cast(fields, @mastery_fields ++ @timestamps)
    |> validate_required(@mastery_fields ++ @timestamps)
  end
end
```

We pipe an empty Response struct through cast to build a changeset, whitelisting the fields we'll accept. Then we pipe that through validate_required to make sure all of the data is correct.

We recognize there's some duplication in this code. That's OK. We think separating the concerns of saving a response and operating a timed quiz is a good idea. Inevitably, the needs of the persistence layer and our Mastery boundary will diverge. Rather than bloating the model to support both concerns, we need only maintain a function doing a transformation between the two.

Establish an API

Let's move on to the main API at lib/mastery_persistence.ex. For this project, our API exists to save and fetch items from a SQL database. For the most part our API will consist of Ecto queries that collect and aggregate responses in various ways.

Where Are the Layers?

 You might be asking yourself, "Where are all of the layers?" In this case, almost the whole project is boundary code. In a database, it's nearly impossible to do anything without side effects. You could call Ecto schemas core functions, but those tiny slices of code are not enough to justify another layer of ceremony by adding one more directory in lib.

It's time to open up lib/mastery_persistence.ex to actually save and query our responses:

Persistence/mastery_persistence/lib/mastery_persistence.ex
```elixir
defmodule MasteryPersistence do
  import Ecto.Query, only: [from: 2]
  alias MasteryPersistence.{Response, Repo}
```

We import Ecto.Query and alias our Repo and Response modules because this file will exist to provide a SQL-focused API to access Mastery responses. Now, we can insert changes into the database, like this:

Persistence/mastery_persistence/lib/mastery_persistence.ex
```elixir
def record_response(response, in_transaction \\ fn _response -> :ok end) do
  {:ok, result} = Repo.transaction(fn ->
    %{
      quiz_title: to_string(response.quiz_title),
      template_name: to_string(response.template_name),
      to: response.to,
      email: response.email,
      answer: response.answer,
      correct: response.correct,
      inserted_at: response.timestamp,
      updated_at: response.timestamp
    }
    |> Response.record_changeset
    |> Repo.insert!
    in_transaction.(response)
  end)
  result
end
```

This function takes raw fields, pipes them through our function to create a changeset and then we save the result to the database.

We also provide an API so that a teacher or an admin can get a report of responses, like so:

Persistence/mastery_persistence/lib/mastery_persistence.ex
```elixir
  def report(quiz_title) do
    quiz_title = to_string(quiz_title)
    from(
      r in Response,
      select: {r.email, count(r.id)},
      where: r.quiz_title == ^quiz_title,
      group_by: [r.quiz_title, r.email]
    )
    |> Repo.all
    |> Enum.into(Map.new)
  end
end
```

We select email and a count(id) column, filter by our quiz title and group by email to give a rough feel for the performance of each individual student. It's a simple grouping of responses by group title, and we're done.

We created our schema and backed it with a repo. All that remains is to build out our final database tables. We'll do that through a migration.

Build Your Postgres Table

Our migration will only require a single table, and we don't need any special behaviors. Create your initial migration with mix, like this:

```
→ mix ecto.gen.migration create_responses
* creating priv/repo/migrations
* creating priv/repo/migrations/20190504175500_create_responses.exs
```

Open up the migration you created. Your name will be a little different from ours due to the date in the filename. Key in this file:

```
defmodule MasteryPersistence.Repo.Migrations.CreateResponses do
  use Ecto.Migration

  def change do
    create table(:responses) do
      add :quiz_title, :string, null: false
      add :template_name, :string, null: false
      add :to, :text, null: false
      add :email, :string, null: false
      add :answer, :string, null: false
      add :correct, :boolean, null: false

      timestamps()
    end

    create index(:responses, :email)
  end
end
```

We create a Postgres table called :responses with the fields we need. Use it to create your database and run the test and development migrations, like this:

```
→ mix ecto.create
→ mix ecto.migrate

→ MIX_ENV=test mix ecto.create
→ MIX_ENV=test mix ecto.migrate
```

The migration works! We have a working persistence back end. It's not yet woven into Mastery, but the integration may be easer than you might think.

Integrate MasteryPersistence into Mastery

Now, it's time to finish up the integration. First, let's think about what needs to happen for Mastery to work with our tiny external persistence project. We'll specify the dependency and modify QuizSession.answer_question to take an extra configurable function, one that will actually persist a response. Here's our checklist:

- Configure the project to use a repository.
- Add a perstence function to our external API.
- Wire that persistence function into the Boundary.QuizSession GenServer.

It's going to go quickly. Let's do the configuration first.

Configure Mastery for Persistence

The first step of our integration is adding the repository to our configuration. To us, the repository is just an external GenServer dependency. Switch over to the mastery directory so we can work on the mother ship. Go to config/config.exs to add the repo, like this:

```
config :mastery_persistence,
    ecto_repos: [MasteryPersistence.Repo]

config :logger, level: :info
```

Simple enough. We configure the :ecto_repos for the new dependency. We'll also need to configure our dev environment, so go to config/dev.exs and add the credentials for our development database like this:

```
use Mix.Config

    config :mastery_persistence, MasteryPersistence.Repo,
      database: "mastery_dev",
      hostname: "localhost"

    config :mastery, :persistence_fn, &MasteryPersistence.record_response/2
```

We configure the database for the integrated app. Notice we're also providing the database function that Mastery will use to save responses. We'll consume this function in a callback API a few steps later.

Next, we want to configure the test environment to use a sandbox environment that rolls back new changes after every test, speeding up our test cases substantially:

config/test.exs

```
use Mix.Config

    config :mastery_persistence, MasteryPersistence.Repo,
      database: "mastery_test",
      hostname: "localhost",
      pool: Ecto.Adapters.SQL.Sandbox
```

We provide the database credentials, making sure the pool uses the Ecto sandbox. Next, we add the dependencies. From mix.exs, add this dependency:

```
{:mastery_persistence, path: "../mastery_persistence"}
```

We're using a poncho-style project. That means our dependencies will use relative paths. With the ceremony out of the way, we can integrate that persistence function.

Integrate a Function to Persist Records

For this feature, let's go from the outside in, addressing the outer API layer first. That way we can think about the shape of our external APIs.

In lib/mastery.ex, we need to pull a persistence function from the environment to dictate the persistence mechanism, like this:

Persistence/lib/mastery.ex
```
@persistence_fn Application.get_env(:mastery, :persistence_fn)
```

Easy enough. We pass in another argument, a function to optionally persist each new response. The responsibility of the function from Mastery's perspective is to return a response. We can use it any way we want. We might decide to save a response to a database or file, or do nothing at all.

We will optionally pass our new function to the QuizSession.answer_question/3 function, like this:

Persistence/lib/mastery.ex
```
def answer_question(name, answer, persistence_fn \\ @persistence_fn) do
  QuizSession.answer_question(name,  answer, persistence_fn)
end
```

This code maintains backward compatibility by providing a default function. If no persistence function is specified, either in the environment or the configuration, our default persistence function *will do nothing*. Any external client code will continue to work and our tests won't need modification.

Let's write that new function we called from mastery.ex api. Open up lib/mastery/boundary/quiz_session.ex and tweak the answer_question message, like this:

```
Persistence/lib/mastery/boundary/quiz_session.ex
def answer_question(name, answer, persistence_fn) do
  GenServer.call(via(name), {:answer_question, answer, persistence_fn})
end
```

This is the ninja move, the place we finally consume the persistence function. Rather than piping a quiz to answer_question and select_question, we do those things in a function. The developer can build a persistence function to save the response to a database or file. Alternatively, the developer can choose to invoke the function and do nothing with the response.

All that remains is to wrap our function in the boundary API. Add the new argument to the QuizSession.answer_question/3 function, like this:

```
Persistence/lib/mastery/boundary/quiz_session.ex
def handle_call({:answer_question, answer, fun}, _from, {quiz, email}) do
  fun = fun || fn r, f -> f.(r) end
  response = Response.new(quiz, email, answer)
  fun.(response, fn r ->
    quiz
    |> Quiz.answer_question(r)
    |> Quiz.select_question
  end)
  |> maybe_finish(email)
end
```

If the user passes in a persistence function, we'll use that one. Otherwise, we take a function which effectively returns the response.

That was easy! Now we can codify the right persistence strategy for persistence. Recall that we configured the database configuration and persistence functions in config and *nothing else needs to change*. You can specify this configuration any way you would like, depending on the configuration needs of your project.

Notice that it would be easy to integrate persistence within our boundary layer. The files and code are exactly the same. Only the configuration would change.

Now that we've seen how to tackle the tricky issues of persistence in a separate dependency, let's look at how we might use these layering strategies within some of Elixir's more popular frameworks, including LiveView and Scenic.

Integrate Your OTP Dependencies into Phoenix

Phoenix is a web framework. Once any web project grows beyond the most rudimentary level of complexity, you're going to need to deal with complexity. We've been clear with the layers that make up any internal component. In this section, we'll discuss how to think about your code organization when you need to plug in to someone else's organization.

By now, you are familiar with the coding guidelines for layers that this book promotes. You are doubtlessly wondering how to integrate OTP code into Phoenix. Here's the good news. Like all Elixir projects built with Mix, OTP is already built in! If you want to integrate a full and separate OTP project, you have a couple of options at your disposal: dependencies, umbrellas, or contexts.

Use External Git or Hex Dependencies

The first approach is to build a fully isolated mix project and use mix dependencies to deal with them. It's a strategy that we've promoted strongly within these pages. To use this technique, you'll build a full independent OTP component you can integrate with other projects.

Since Phoenix is itself an OTP framework, integration is straightforward. Throughout Part II of this book, we've shown you how to organize and integrate your boundary, and how to make a simple API available to other programs. You need only configure your project:

1. Register your dependencies in mix.exs
2. Configure your supervisors in application.exs
3. Provide any project-specific configuration (for example, the persistence configuration in Mastery)

We've covered these first two steps fairly exhaustively throughout this book. In terms of how to make your dependencies available, we're going to examine several different approaches, starting with the greatest separation and working toward the most integrated. We'll address external dependencies, umbrella projects, and file organization techniques.

Let's start with external dependencies. Through the mix deps[1] configuration, you can publish a public or private Hex dependency or access your project as a direct git dependency. So far, most of the dependencies in this book have been Hex dependencies, meaning the code comes from a centralized repository called Hex. Git dependencies look like this:

```
{:gettext, git: "https://github.com/elixir-lang/gettext.git", tag: "0.1"}
```

This dependency will fetch the dependency from github.com instead of hex.pm. The benefits of using fully external git or hex dependencies are all around

---

1. https://hexdocs.pm/mix/Mix.Tasks.Deps.html

reduced coupling. You can work with each project with complete isolation. For this reason, when you're working with something like microservices in Elixir, external dependencies are the perfect choice. You're forced to think hard about your external interfaces and get them right.

There's a drawback, though. From a workflow perspective, if a dependency is not yet mature, working with independent repositories does have a cost. It's more labor intensive because you need a separate workflow to publish each dependency when you change it. These kinds of dependencies are also less forgiving when you get your major interface boundaries wrong. For that reason, it's usually best to start with a slightly more integrated approach such as ponchos and then extract projects to external dependencies once those interfaces mature.

Use External Path Dependencies

If you want to work with an external dependency but want the convenience of keeping everything in the same repository, you can take the same approach we did with persistence and use a poncho-style dependency. Poncho dependencies have an ever-so-slight coupling to their parent projects, an organizational coupling.

The benefits are development independence with reduced ceremony. You'll be able to evolve interfaces side by side. Since all of your dependencies are in the same repository, you'll be able to better keep them in sync.

There's also a downside to path dependencies with respect to tooling. There's no automated way to build and test an entire project, dependencies and all. If tooling becomes a burden, you can go with an umbrella dependency.

Use Umbrella Projects

Like poncho projects, umbrella mix projects[2] integrate dependencies in a single repository. Umbrella projects also have another benefit: they let developers both work on each project independently and do selected tasks project wide. For example, using umbrellas you can choose to run tests for all projects with a single command or switch into a single project and run only those tests.

Umbrellas have that tooling advantage, and it's nice. When it's easy to run tests across all projects, those tests will get run more often before checkin.

---

2. https://elixir-lang.org/getting-started/mix-otp/dependencies-and-umbrella-projects.html

That's important if you're not running some kind of automated test when you commit code.

There's a significant downside, though. *Umbrellas must share all dependencies.* That means when you upgrade a single dependency for one project, you must upgrade it for all. As the surface area for the combined umbrella projects increases, this burden can get more and more daunting.

The benefits and weaknesses might be speaking to you. Your dependency strategies all decrease development time ceremony to varying degrees, at the expense of various degrees of coupling. Let's look at one final piece of the puzzle, Phoenix contexts.

Contexts Decrease Ceremony and Increase Coupling

The Phoenix documentation defines contexts like this: "Contexts are dedicated modules that expose and group related functionality." In other words, contexts look much like the top level Mastery module we've built in this book. Contexts serve the same purpose that our API modules serve for our OTP projects. In fact, all of the advice that we provide in this book can apply to a Phoenix context.

If you want to know more, the book *Programming Phoenix 1.4 [TV19]* has a good discussion of how to use contexts. Since Elixir creator José Valim and Phoenix creator Chris McCord are on the author byline for that book, you can trust the advice you get there.

In the next section, we'll go beyond integrating dependencies and walk you through the strategies you can use for integrating into OTP projects. While the task might seem daunting, it's not as tricky as you think.

Organize Code for OTP Abstractions

A growing number of Elixir projects are allowing library integration by making OTP callbacks, or something like them, directly available to developers. In the next few pages, we'll suggest how you might integrate our layers into those frameworks. We'll cover Phoenix Channels, Phoenix LiveView, and Scenic. Once you know how these work, you'll have a pretty good idea of how to integrate with other callback-style frameworks.

Even if you don't have experience with any of these frameworks, allow us a moment to offer a few clues that will help you recognize where the main integration points might be for each section. Once you can recognize those integration points, you'll know how to tie in to the rest of the layers in your project. In each case, the key will be to find where each library exposes call-backs from within an OTP GenServer.

Understand Callback-Style Libraries

If you want to use a simple mix project as a dependency, whether it's an OTP project or a simple library, you don't care about the callback structure. Sometimes, though, you'll want to replace the boundary layer in Chapter 6, Isolate Process Machinery in a Boundary, on page 101 with one wired directly to the framework you're using. The GenServer behaviour has at least two pieces of functionality any framework needs to wrap:

A way to start a process
> GenServer calls these functions within process start machinery. The formal GenServer behaviour has both a start_link function and an init function.

A way to process a callback
> GenServers invoke these callbacks in the machinery that receives messages. The GenServer behaviour has at least three callbacks that are interesting to us, including handle_call, handle_cast, and handle_info.

For convenience, we also wrapped our callbacks in functions, but don't let that distract you. Startup and callbacks are the pieces you want to look for. Once you identify those pieces, then incorporating an event-based library is easy. Let's see a couple of examples, starting with Phoenix Channels.

Add Layers to Phoenix Channels

Phoenix Channels[3] is a great way to build interactive applications, using JavaScript. We won't try to cover this framework exhaustively, only the parts related to the integration of OTP applications. Briefly, it works like this.

- The developer configures Phoenix using some kind of transport. For convenience, let's say the user is using websockets.[4]

- On the client, the developer establishes communication with Phoenix by opening a websocket connection on a particular *channel*, meaning all communication covering a topic of interest for that user.

- On the server, the developer implements the code for that channel using a callback library.

---

3. https://hexdocs.pm/phoenix/channels.html
4. https://en.wikipedia.org/wiki/WebSocket

We won't get into the client side JavaScript or all of the layers of configuration between the client and the channel implementation. You'll find better sources of information in the Hex documentation for Channels[5] listed previously and *Programming Phoenix 1.4 [TV19]*. We'll focus instead on the integration points for OTP.

Generally speaking, coding a channel looks much like coding an OTP boundary layer. Here's an example from the documentation cited previously. First, here's how a user would join a channel:

```
defmodule HelloWeb.RoomChannel do
  use Phoenix.Channel

  def join("room:lobby", _message, socket) do
    {:ok, socket}
  end
end
```

Though it may not look like it, this code is a GenServer! The base implementation is inside Phoenix.Channel. Think of this code as the combination of start_link and init. When the client calls the web socket and asks to join a channel with the topic room:lobby, Phoenix invokes the callback join with a topic, a message, and a socket. Think of the socket as the initial state for this GenServer.

Once we've established a connection between a user and their channel, we can send and receive messages. For example, here's an example of a new message in a room:

```
def handle_in("new_msg", %{"body" => body}, socket) do
  broadcast!(socket, "new_msg", %{body: body})
  {:noreply, socket}
end
```

This information looks just like a handle_cast because it *is a handle_cast*. Under the hood, this GenServer is receiving the message for us and giving us a chance to change the state or process side effects. In this case, we want to simply send the message to everyone else subscribed to the topic with the broadcast! function.

There are other functions to give Phoenix users the ability to send and receive messages, but these are the basics. In OTP, you start a process with a start_link and then process callbacks as they come in with handle_call, handle_cast, and the like. With Phoenix, you start a process with join and process callbacks with handle_in, handle_out, and the like.

---

5.   https://hexdocs.pm/phoenix/channels.html

Here's the point. Since you already know how to use OTP, using Phoenix does not change the way we structure our layers one bit. If we'd decided to implement Mastery as a pure Phoenix application, our design would look very much the same as it does right now. We'd have a few tweaks based on Phoenix capabilities and the use case, but we'd still have the same exact layers. We'd just replace the SessionServer with a SessionChannel, and that Channel module would accept the exact same messages, though we might not choose to wrap those handle calls in a public API.

We should point out that it would be perfectly valid to maintain our Mastery project exactly as it is, and use it as a dependency rather than breaking out the individual callbacks in the boundary layer, and to use the various public Mastery.x functions within, perhaps, QuizChannel and QuizBuilderChannel.

Let's move on to a few other implementations. You'll find the story very much the same.

Add Layers to LiveView

Since LiveView is an implementation of Phoenix Channels, the integration story for the two frameworks is going to be similar. Phoenix LiveView[6] is a library for allowing highly interactive applications with impressive performance and bidirectional communication. That sounds much like Channels, but there's an important distinction. LiveView does so with no custom JavaScript!

Here's how it works:

1. The developer configures LiveView, including integrating some OTP dependencies and a common JavaScript library. (Don't worry. As promised, you'll not use JavaScript in the day-to-day coding of your project.)

2. The infrastructure calls a mount point when a user connects to start a new GenServer process the first time.

3. A server-side function renders a user interface using the state and templates.

4. The framework JavaScript automatically sends messages to the server, which the server translates to GenServer callbacks.

5. When those callbacks fire, LiveView sends any state changes back to the client, resulting in a fresh page in the browser.

---

6. https://github.com/phoenixframework/phoenix_live_view

Watching a highly interactive web page built with LiveView is really quite a spectacle, but implementing them is quite simple. Here are a few relevant snippets of LiveView details from the main project's documentation. It's an implementation of a Thermostat.

First, this mount function establishes a new process when the user loads a LiveView:

```
defmodule AppWeb.ThermostatLive do
  use Phoenix.LiveView

  def mount(%{id: id, current_user_id: user_id}, socket) do
    case Thermostat.get_user_reading(user_id, id) do
      {:ok, temperature} ->
        {:ok, assign(socket, :temperature, temperature)}
      {:error, reason} ->
        {:error, reason}
    end
  end
end
```

OK, there's your start link. Loading a LiveView calls mount, passing an initial message and the initial state of socket, particularly the temperature field within the assigns map that resides in socket. Then, changes come in on handle_event, like this:

```
def handle_event("inc_temperature", _value, socket) do
  {:ok, new_temp} = Thermostat.inc_temperature(socket.assigns.id)
  {:noreply, assign(socket, :temperature, new_temp)}
end
```

We increment the temperature on the thermostat and then set socket.assigns.temperature with the new :temperature. Now all that remains is to update the view. Implicitly, every call to handle_event also calls render on that LiveView. Let's show a bare-bones user interface, like this:

```
def render(assigns) do
  ~L\"""
  Current temperature: <%= @temperature %>
  \"""
end
```

The render/1 function takes one argument, socket.assigns, which is where Phoenix keeps all user data within a socket. The function is a straight template, with two slight customizations. The ~L""" sigil represents the heart of the LiveView module, and provides a shorthand way to modify the template for LiveView's needs. <%= @temperature %> is a shorthand directive for doing a substitution.

And that's it. As with Phoenix Channels, this example has the right shape to plug straight into our boundary layer. Since this structure *is* a channel and *is* an OTP GenServer, all of the organizational techniques we've presented to layer your code still work.

There's one last framework to visit. Let's take a quick look at Scenic.

Build Scenic Projects with Layers

Scenic is an Elixir library that builds native user interfaces. Like Channels and LiveView for Phoenix, Scenic is an OTP callback-based library. A Scenic Scene is a GenServer process which creates and manages a Graph that gets drawn to the screen. You can possibly already see where this is going. This is how it all works:

1. At initialization, a scene creates a Graph module, one with the buttons, text, and other features that make up a user interface.

2. Events from the user interface come into scenes as GenServer messages, which can change the graphs or other custom state.

3. Event callbacks can optionally render the scene.

The initialization is like the start link; the events are GenServer callbacks; and the render code is just a function. Conceptually, that's what's happening with the other frameworks we talked about. Let's take a quick look at at a trivial Scenic app:

```
defmodule MyApp.Scene.Example do
  use Scenic.Scene
  alias Scenic.Graph
  alias Scenic.Primitives
  alias Scenic.Components
```

We use Scenic.Scene, which bring in the GenServer features among other things. We alias Scenic.Graph so we can build the graph having the instructions to build our user interface. The GenServer process will hold that graph. Then we import the primitives and controls so we can use Scenic within module.

Now we can build the initial graph in a module attribute like this:

```
@graph Graph.build()
  |> Primitives.text("Hello World", font_size: 16, translate: {20, 80})
  |> Components.button({"Big Button", :button}, translate: {20, 180})
```

We build a default scene and then add some text and a button. Then we can initialize the graph.

```
def init( scene, _options ) do
  {:ok, @graph, push: @graph}
end

...

end
```

We implement our initial callback, init. This function takes the arguments for a scene and options. In Scenic terminology, the push: @graph option pushes the data to the viewport, making it available to the user.

This code fills all of the requirements to be a working scene. Let's get a little more sophisticated by building the skeleton of a hypothetical game. To periodically update the game at specific intervals, we can send a timer event to our scene with Erlang's timer, like this:

```
def init( _scene, _options ) do
  {:ok, timer} = :timer.send_interval(@ms_to_next_frame, :update_frame)
  ...
  {:ok, @game, push: @initial_game}
end
```

Since a scene is a GenServer, we can send messages using any mechanism that we want. Now, we can update the user interface in @game by processing an inbound callback, like this:

```
def handle_info(:update_frame, %{frame_count: frame_count} = game) do
  game = update_game(game)

  game.graph
  |> draw_game(game.objects)
  |> push_graph()

  {:noreply, %{game | frame_count: frame_count + 1}}
end
```

You may recognize handle_info as a GenServer callback, and it is. The only Scenic-specific code here is between the do and the return tuple. We take our game graph, update it with a function called draw_game and then pipe that to push_graph, a Scenic function that renders the graph to your chosen hardware. Conceptually, all that remains is to process input. You can do so with one of a number of messages Scenic supports, such as this one to receive key presses:

```
def handle_input({:key, {"left", :press, _}}, _context, game) do
  {:noreply, update_pacman_direction(game, {-1, 0})}
end

def handle_input({:key, {"up", :press, _}}, _context, game) do
  {:noreply, update_pacman_direction(game, {0, -1})}
end

...
```

We take a message that's an inbound keypress and update the state of the game based on the keypress. You can see the messages for a left key and an up key, which should show you the idea. Then, you could implement the update_game function to move the game token based on the direction.

While Scenic has some features that may be new to you, the organization of the layers is right in line with what you already know. The scene is a boundary layer with some additional machinery to represent and render user interfaces, based on state. Our GenServer behind the curtain provides a message loop we can use to update game state. If you'd like to see the game that provided the rough inspiration for this example, check out this excellent writeup for building the classic snake[7] game.

Assemble Your Components

In this chapter we showed how components work together. Starting a project with abstract structs rather than immediately into persistence give us some tangible benefits. The biggest one was having a bigger functional core and a smaller boundary. Building in persistence at that point allowed us to reduce coupling between the base OTP component and the database schema. To illustrate that benefit, we have implemented persistence as a straight path dependency.

Building MasteryPersistence with path dependencies let us isolate implementations into separate projects without the additional ceremony of maintaining separate repositories. Git and Hex dependencies offer their own trade-offs, providing reduced coupling at the cost of additional ceremony. On the other side of the coin, building in umbrellas or contexts made the opposite trade-offs, offering less ceremony at the cost of tighter coupling.

Elixir provides a wide slate of solutions for consuming libraries and OTP applications. One such solution is callback-style integration. It's a strategy that is growing in popularity in many of the most powerful OTP frameworks. Phoenix Channels, Phoenix LiveView, and Scenic all offer frameworks for rendering user interfaces. A project implementing any of those solutions works well with the layers presented in this book. In each case, the solution is to replace the boundary layer with the GenServer-specific module that implements callbacks, a Channel, LiveView, or Scene.

---

7. https://blog.usejournal.com/elixir-scenic-snake-game-b8616b1d7ee0

If you're like us, you might feel a little nervous when you implement so much code without having the tests to show for it. Now that we've built out our boundary layer and examined strategies to integrate our components, it's time to test the GenServers.

Our tests will give us a great opportunity to provide a more cohesive view of how the APIs work together. It's time for the big finish!

CHAPTER 10

Test the Boundary

We've finally reached the last chapter of this book. We're going to test the boundary layers of Mastery, the "big loud worker-bees" words of our sentence. These layers deal with the boundary API, lifecycles, and workers. As a bonus, we'll also test the external component we introduced in Chapter 9, Assemble Your Components, on page 173.

As we work through our tests, we'll need to deal with some complex issues that were not on the table when we tested the relatively pure core layers in Chapter 5, Test Your Core, on page 75. Luckily, our layering system means we won't have to repeat the core-centered tests of the pure business logic. We'll focus on the complexity of the machinery dealing with processes, timing, and external interfaces.

Mastery has some of the same interesting testing challenges you'll find in many other systems. We'll focus on three of them.

A common integration testing layer allows a test to exercise a codebase just as an end user would, at least with respect to the way it executes code. We'll write such a test for Mastery's boundary layers.

We won't stop testing persistence at the base Mastery API, though. We'll be sure to test the basic usage of our external poncho project and work in some coverage of error conditions at the same time.

Testing intricately timed code often provides specific challenges for testers. We'll wrap things up by doing some slight modifications to Mastery to enable a better testing experience. Then, we'll wrap up this entire project.

Along the way, you should get a better sense of the API we've created and how to use it in a project. We know you're excited, so we'll get right to the code.

Tests Call the API as a User Would

Our test will deal with the entire Mastery API. This whole book has been building up to this point. This test will not exercise our code as an interior function might, rather, it will test the whole API as an end user of the dependency. If we've done our job well, we'll be able to express the entire test in a few short pages of code.

Our plan is to cover tests for the overarching API, and then move on to more specific tests within the poncho project. In this chapter, we won't provide an exhaustive test to cover every corner condition. Instead, we'll give you the strategies you might use to meet the testing strategies you're likely to face to build effective boundary tests. Let's write the first test.

Test the External API

It's finally time to override the pristine test/mastery_test.exs that mix created when we built the initial Mastery project. This test is designed to exercise the external API that allows access to external dependencies. We'll work from the outside in. Crack it open now:

```
BoundaryTests/test/mastery_test.exs
defmodule MasteryTest do
  use ExUnit.Case, async: false
  use QuizBuilders
  alias MasteryPersistence.Repo
  alias Mastery.Examples.Math
  alias Mastery.Boundary.QuizSession
  alias MasteryPersistence.Response
```

We start with the module definition, the use directive for the ExUnit test case for running tests, and the use directive for our helper fixtures. We establish these tests as async: false because they should not run concurrently. We have a single QuizManager GenServer that's bound to the module so running a concurrent version of this test would interfere with our test. Luckily, this file will be pretty thin so we won't pay too much of a penalty.

We follow our use directives up with more than a few aliases for all of the services we plan to use. It's an integration test, after all. Now, we can turn our attention to persistence:

```
BoundaryTests/test/mastery_test.exs
defp enable_persistence() do
  :ok = Ecto.Adapters.SQL.Sandbox.checkout(Repo)
end
```

Our enable_persistence function will check out an Ecto sandbox database to make sure we get the Repo that manages transactions for us in test mode. Later, when we answer a question, we will specify our persistence function. That way we can leave persistence disabled for most of our tests, but include them when we need to. We want our tests to run quickly, so if a test is not working directly with persistence concerns we don't want the database and its overhead enabled!

With the configuration behind us, we can shift our attention to the implementation of the aggregation we'll need to count responses:

```
BoundaryTests/test/mastery_test.exs
defp response_count() do
  Repo.aggregate(Response, :count, :id)
end
```

This little Ecto one-liner will make it easy for us to count responses and keep the test focused on high-level abstractions. We name the concept well with a descriptive function name to keep our intentions clear.

That's all we need to do for persistence within Mastery. Next, we can move on to the helpers that will let us build and start and take the quiz:

```
BoundaryTests/test/mastery_test.exs
defp start_quiz(fields) do
  now = DateTime.utc_now()
  ending = DateTime.add(now, 60)

  Mastery.schedule_quiz(Math.quiz_fields(), fields, now, ending)
end

defp take_quiz(email) do
  Mastery.take_quiz(Math.quiz.title, email)
end
```

start_quiz schedules the quiz to start immediately with more than enough time to take the quiz. We'll achieve mastery far before the timer runs out. take_quiz lets a user establish a session.

Now we can move on to the helpers to answer a quiz:

```
BoundaryTests/test/mastery_test.exs
defp select_question(session) do
  assert Mastery.select_question(session) == "1 + 2"
end
```

```elixir
defp give_wrong_answer(session) do
  Mastery.answer_question(
    session,
    "wrong",
    &MasteryPersistence.record_response/2
  )
end

defp give_right_answer(session) do
  Mastery.answer_question(
    session,
    "3",
    &MasteryPersistence.record_response/2
  )
end
```

By now, these functions should be pretty familiar. We have a function to select a question and then a couple of functions to provide right and wrong answers. Notice that we provide the persistence function to use for saving the responses. That way, only the tests that use these functions will actually persist responses.

We've already tested the functionality for creating new questions from a template, so our templates will build questions where the right answer is always 3. Now we are ready to do the setup:

BoundaryTests/test/mastery_test.exs
```elixir
setup do
  enable_persistence()

  always_add_1_to_2 =
    [
      template_fields(generators: addition_generators([1], [2]))
    ]

  assert "" != ExUnit.CaptureLog.capture_log(fn ->
    :ok = start_quiz(always_add_1_to_2)
  end)

  :ok
end
```

The setup establishes persistence and then builds the now-familiar templates using our helpers that allow only questions with a specific answer.

Let's shift our attention to the quiz startup. We capture the log so that our "Quiz Starting" log message won't give us noisy testing output. We also run an assertion here to make sure we get a log message.

Finally, we return an :ok atom, which is one of two acceptable responses for ExUnit setup blocks. All that remains is the test itself:

```
BoundaryTests/test/mastery_test.exs
  test "Take a quiz, manage lifecycle and persist responses" do
    session = take_quiz("yes_mathter@example.com")

    select_question(session)
    assert give_wrong_answer(session) == {"1 + 2", false}
    assert give_right_answer(session) == {"1 + 2", true}
    assert response_count() > 0

    assert give_right_answer(session) == :finished
    assert QuizSession.active_sessions_for(Math.quiz_fields().title) == []

  end
end
```

The test itself is almost anticlimactic. We start a session, select a question, answer some questions and then count responses. We don't know for sure that our abstraction is right, but we do know that *if your abstraction is right, your tests should be simple.* We'll take this as a good sign.

We can run our tests now:

```
→ mix test test/mastery_test.exs
.

Finished in 0.06 seconds
1 test, 0 failures
```

We're clean and green! We have packed a ton of functionality into our brief test, but it's a good one. We make a trade-off here. Our test mixes the concerns of lifecycle through processes and persistence, but for a good reason.

We believe that a test is like a scientific experiment. It does something using the codebase and then makes a series of measurements. In ExUnit, those experiments are function calls and the measurements are assertions. We're not terribly concerned about mixing several different kinds of assertions in the same test, especially for tests that are pretty expensive in terms of time.

It's a trade-off though. If you value decoupling of these concerns more than time, feel free to separate the database and lifecycle portions of this test. The structure of the codebase will make this separation easy to do.

The relatively short test also shows how simple it is to attach optional persistence with this method. We've effectively built a solution that lets us turn persistence on and off with a few short lines of code. For the right problem, this approach is a boon that allows multiple persistence approaches within the same codebase. For Mastery, this approach will pay dividends should we want to build a web-based practice front end without involving the database, while still allowing a full featured front end that supports reporting in the classroom.

Our tests are not enough, though. We need to isolate the most complex elements of our boundary and test those layers independently. Let's dive into the test for our poncho project and build some basic tests for MasteryPersistence, ones that cover basic corner cases such as error conditions.

Test Poncho Projects Directly

As we build our poncho dependencies, they'll need testing just like our other solutions do. Testing is especially important for boundary concerns as those code paths will need to embrace the chaos inherent in external dependencies, timing-based error conditions, and the complexity inherent in systems that allow mutability. Boundaries encapsulate many of the properties that make our programs the most useful.

MasteryPersistence is a pretty shallow codebase that has a pretty clear API for its most important features. We'll focus all of our energy testing that API. We'll put all of our tests in a single file, understanding that we can break up that file should we need to do so.

Since the project doesn't have a complex schema, we won't need to build any test fixtures for it. We'll be able to get away with a basic setup for all tests and then independent tests for each concept we want to test.

Crack open mastery_persistence/test/mastery_persistence_test.exs and key this in. We'll follow the entire flow and then run the tests:

BoundaryTests/mastery_persistence/test/mastery_persistence_test.exs
```
defmodule MasteryPersistenceTest do
  use ExUnit.Case

  alias MasteryPersistence.{Response, Repo}
```

We start with the basic ceremony, the code that defines the module, fires the use directive to enable ExUnit test cases and includes the parts of MasteryPersistence that we intend to consume. Moving on to the setup code:

```
BoundaryTests/mastery_persistence/test/mastery_persistence_test.exs
setup do
  :ok = Ecto.Adapters.SQL.Sandbox.checkout(Repo)
  response = %{
    quiz_title: :simple_addition,
    template_name: :single_digit_addition,
    to: "3 + 4",
    email: "student@example.com",
    answer: "7",
    correct: true,
    timestamp: DateTime.utc_now
  }
  {:ok, %{response: response}}
end
```

The setup code enables our Ecto test repo to establish test-style transactions
and creates a basic response for us to use. Now, we can move on to the individual tests. First, we'll test the function that persists response structs
directly:

```
BoundaryTests/mastery_persistence/test/mastery_persistence_test.exs
test "responses are recorded", %{response: response} do
  assert Repo.aggregate(Response, :count, :id) == 0
  assert :ok = MasteryPersistence.record_response(response)
  assert Repo.all(Response)
         |> Enum.map(fn r -> r.email end) == [response.email]
end
```

This test makes sure our table is empty and then fires the underlying persistence mechanism, the record_response/1 function. Finally, we make sure the
function in fact records responses with a simple aggregate call to our Repo that
counts distinct :id values.

With that much behind us, we can test the feature that persists responses
through a user-defined function, the same one Mastery uses:

```
BoundaryTests/mastery_persistence/test/mastery_persistence_test.exs
test "a function can be run in the saving transaction",
    %{response: response} do
  assert response.answer ==
         MasteryPersistence.record_response(response, fn r -> r.answer end)
end
```

We fire the MasteryPersistence.record_response/2 function, passing it a simple function
returning a response. We assert that the answer property matches the one we
passed in.

With the base cases behind us, we can exercise the corner cases, starting with error conditions:

```
BoundaryTests/mastery_persistence/test/mastery_persistence_test.exs
test "an error in the function rolls back the save",
    %{response: response} do
  assert Repo.aggregate(Response, :count, :id) == 0
  assert_raise RuntimeError, fn ->
    MasteryPersistence.record_response(response, fn _r -> raise "oops" end)
  end
  assert Repo.aggregate(Response, :count, :id) == 0
end
```

In this test, we use the ExUnit assert_raise function and pass it a code block. Notice the anonymous function we pass to record_response intentionally raises an error. After calling the record_response function, we make sure that no responses are saved once again with Repo.aggregate.

We can smell the finish line. We need only do a rudimentary function to test out our persistence reporting feature, like this:

```
BoundaryTests/mastery_persistence/test/mastery_persistence_test.exs
  test "simple reporting", %{response: response} do
    MasteryPersistence.record_response(response)
    MasteryPersistence.record_response(response)

    response
    |> Map.put(:email, "other_#{response.email}")
    |> MasteryPersistence.record_response

    assert MasteryPersistence.report(response.quiz_title) == %{
      response.email => 2,
      "other_#{response.email}" => 1
    }
  end
end
```

We record a few responses and then check the results of the reporting against expectations. We're done!

We can run our tests independently of the rest of Mastery. Let's change into the mastery_persistence directory and then run tests, like this:

```
➜ cd mastery_persistence
➜ mix test
....

Finished in 0.07 seconds
4 tests, 0 failures
```

Everything works! The tests are not quite as simple as they would have been had we integrated persistence into Mastery, but the benefit for our use case is worth it, as we can determine which persistence back end is best for our users.

We have one last feature to test, the proctor. Since it has some timing related features, it will have some particularly strong challenges for us.

Isolate the Proctor's Boundary Concerns

In many ways, our proctor is the biggest testing challenge in this book. We have a scheduler that depends on concepts of both mutability and time, ideas that are generally kryptonite for tests.

The scheduler has three events: schedule, start quiz, and stop quiz. Each of these ideas is important. Our tests could wait, using sleeps, as our quizzes cycle through their respective states, but that strategy would make our tests both fragile and slow.

Sleeps in tests are inherently bad. Wait too long and your tests are slow; don't wait long enough and your tests won't be consistent. To prevent race conditions and timing dependent code, we'll need to find a better approach.

Here's our plan, then. Let's modify our code to allow custom notifications when important things happen, namely when a quiz starts and finishes. Our tests can then await an event instead of sleeping for some specific amount of time.

The bonus is that by building in this new feature, our project will be better as it's precisely the kind of feature that user interfaces will need to keep our customers informed.

In detail, this is what we'll do. In Mastery, we will:

1. Add an optional process ID to `Mastery.schedule_quiz`
2. Modify the Proctor to accept this new argument
3. Notify the specified process when a quiz starts
4. Notify the process when a quiz stops

When we are done, our tests will be much simpler. They will need only await these specific messages as they work their way through the test. Let us do that now.

Add a Notification to Mastery and the Boundary

We'll start with lib/mastery.ex to make the API changes, and then we'll enable that new API in the boundary. In Mastery, we need to change the API to accept our new notify_pid, like this:

BoundaryTests/lib/mastery.ex
```
def schedule_quiz(quiz, templates, start_at, end_at, notify_pid \\ nil) do
  with :ok <- QuizValidator.errors(quiz),
       true <- Enum.all?(templates, &(:ok == TemplateValidator.errors(&1))),
       :ok <-
         Proctor.schedule_quiz(
           quiz,
           templates,
           start_at,
           end_at,
           notify_pid),
  do: :ok, else: (error -> error)
end
```

That's simple enough. We add a new optional argument to schedule_quiz and pass it straight through to the proctor. We'll make the notify_pid optional here so the change will be compatible.

With the easy part behind us, we need to make this new API work on the back end. Open up lib/mastery/boundary/proctor.ex, and add the new argument to schedule_quiz, like this:

BoundaryTests/lib/mastery/boundary/proctor.ex
```
def schedule_quiz(
  proctor \\ __MODULE__,
  quiz,
  temps,
  start_at,
  end_at,
  notify_pid) do
  quiz = %{
    fields: quiz,
    templates: temps,
    start_at: start_at,
    end_at: end_at,
    notify_pid: notify_pid,
  }
  GenServer.call(proctor, {:schedule_quiz, quiz})
end
```

We add the new argument and pass it through to the handle_call callback as a quiz map key. Though it won't need any changes, let's refresh our memory of the handle_call function for add_quiz in the GenServer:

```
BoundaryTests/lib/mastery/boundary/proctor.ex
def handle_call({:schedule_quiz, quiz}, _from, quizzes) do
  now = DateTime.utc_now
  ordered_quizzes =
    [quiz | quizzes]
    |> start_quizzes(now)
    |> Enum.sort(fn a, b ->
      date_time_less_than_or_equal?(a.start_at, b.start_at)
    end)
  build_reply_with_timeout({:reply, :ok}, ordered_quizzes, now)
end
```

Notice that our quiz already has the notify built in so we don't need to make any changes. We can jump straight to the implementation of start_quizzes:

```
BoundaryTests/lib/mastery/boundary/proctor.ex
defp start_quizzes(quizzes, now) do
  {ready, not_ready} = Enum.split_while(quizzes, fn quiz ->
    date_time_less_than_or_equal?(quiz.start_at, now)
  end )
  Enum.each(ready, fn quiz -> start_quiz(quiz, now) end)
  not_ready
end
```

Once again, passing the details through as a quiz key has saved us one more interface change.

Let's add the notification to start_quiz:

```
BoundaryTests/lib/mastery/boundary/proctor.ex
def start_quiz(quiz, now) do
  Logger.info "Starting quiz #{quiz.fields.title}..."
  notify_start(quiz)
  QuizManager.build_quiz(quiz.fields)
  Enum.each(quiz.templates, &add_template(quiz, &1))
  timeout = DateTime.diff(quiz.end_at, now, :millisecond)
  Process.send_after(
    self(),
    {:end_quiz, quiz.fields.title, quiz.notify_pid},
    timeout)
end
```

In start_quiz, we have two changes to make. First, after we log the start of the quiz, we call our new notify_start function where we'll actually do the notification via send. Next, scan down to the message we send in Process.send_after. We don't send the whole quiz to that message so we add the notify_pid as the third part of that message tuple.

Now we can finally do the first notification, the one that happens when a quiz starts:

BoundaryTests/lib/mastery/boundary/proctor.ex
```
defp notify_start(%{notify_pid: nil}), do: nil
defp notify_start(quiz) do
  send(quiz.notify_pid, {:started, quiz.fields.title})
end
```

In the first clause, there's nothing to do if there's no pid. In the second head, we match the pid and then we actually send the notification message via send.

Now we need to adjust our message for the :end_quiz, and actually do the notification there:

BoundaryTests/lib/mastery/boundary/proctor.ex
```
def handle_info({:end_quiz, title, notify_pid}, quizzes) do
  QuizManager.remove_quiz(title)
  title
  |> QuizSession.active_sessions_for
  |> QuizSession.end_sessions
  Logger.info "Stopped quiz #{title}."
  notify_stopped(notify_pid, title)
  handle_info(:timeout, quizzes)
end
```

All we need to do is to accept the additional element in the :end_quiz message tuple and then call the notification. Once again, the point where we do the logging is ideal. The function to do the work looks much like the one for start_quiz:

BoundaryTests/lib/mastery/boundary/proctor.ex
```
  defp notify_stopped(nil, _title), do: nil
  defp notify_stopped(pid, title), do: send(pid, {:stopped, title})
end
```

If there's no pid, there's nothing to do. If there's a pid, we send a tuple with the :stopping_quiz atom and the title of the quiz. We're almost ready to write the tests, but first let's verify that all of our new code actually works.

Work with the New Notifications

To review, rather than jumping straight into our tests with sleeps and timing dependent code, we built a quick feature that our tests can use. Other programs can take advantage of notifications too. Let's test that theory with the IEx program. Fire it up with iex -S mix. Then, type this much:

```
iex(1)> alias Mastery.Examples.Math
Mastery.Examples.Math
```

We alias the Math example so we can use those fields to create our quiz and templates. Next, we can do a little date math, like this:

```
iex(2)> now = DateTime.utc_now()
#DateTime<2019-06-30 14:21:53.159751Z>
iex(3)> five_seconds_from_now = DateTime.add(now, 5)
#DateTime<2019-06-30 14:21:58.159751Z>
iex(4)> one_minute_from_now = DateTime.add(now, 60)
#DateTime<2019-06-30 14:22:53.159751Z>
iex(5)> Mastery.schedule_quiz(Mastery.Examples.Math.quiz_fields(),
...(5)> [Math.template_fields()], five_seconds_from_now, one_minute_from_now,
...(5)> self())
```

We schedule a quiz with some times relative to now. You may have to adjust the timing of these features to get things to work right for you, but the premise is the same. The first time is now, the second is the time we'll use to start a quiz, and the third is the time the quiz will no longer be available.

Next, we will see the quiz start:

```
10:23:48.562 [info]  Starting quiz simple_addition...
:ok
```

The scheduler is working. Now we can take the quiz, like this:

```
iex(6)> Mastery.take_quiz(Math.quiz_fields().title, "james@graysoftinc.com")
{:simple_addition, "james@graysoftinc.com"}
iex(7)>
10:24:33.560 [info]  Stopped quiz simple_addition.

nil
```

After a minute or so, we had to press Enter. At that point we could see that the quiz had stopped.

If we implemented the notify_pid correctly, we should see a couple of messages in our process message queue, like this:

```
iex(8)> receive do message -> message end
{:started, :simple_addition}
iex(9)> receive do message -> message end
{:stopped, :simple_addition}
```

It works! We get two notifications, one when the Proctor starts the quiz and one when it stops the quiz. Now we have everything we need. We're finally ready to write the tests.

Write the Tests

Once the additional infrastructure of the scheduling notification is in place, our tests will be easier to write. Let's dive right in:

```
BoundaryTests/test/proctor_test.exs
defmodule ProctorTest do
  use ExUnit.Case

  alias Mastery.Examples.Math
  alias Mastery.Boundary.QuizSession

  @moduletag capture_log: true
```

We do the typical setup ceremony, with one addition. With the module attribute @capture_log, we turn on the logging capture so that we won't add noisy logging to our test cases.

The rest of this test case will deal with time. Boundaries are powerful but all of that power has a cost: the ceremony of dealing with time. This test exists specifically to walk our code through its entire lifecycle, step by step. We'll do all of this work in a single test to keep things simple to read and maintain in the future.

The first step is to start up the quiz, like this:

```
BoundaryTests/test/proctor_test.exs
test "quizzes can be scheduled" do
  quiz = Math.quiz_fields |> Map.put(:title, :timed_addition)
  now = DateTime.utc_now
  email = "student@example.com"
```

We declare the test and handle all of the ceremony for a quiz startup, complete with the quiz fields and the initial date math.

The next step is to use those fields to schedule a quiz:

```
BoundaryTests/test/proctor_test.exs
assert :ok == Mastery.schedule_quiz(
  quiz,
  [Math.template_fields],
  DateTime.add(now, 50, :millisecond),
  DateTime.add(now, 100, :millisecond),
  self()
)
```

We call the Mastery.schedule_quiz function to schedule the quiz. We pass in a start time and a stop time, both using fractions of a second. Keep in mind that we're effectively doing a sleep, so we don't want to do too many of these in our test cases, but this test is only burning up a tenth of a second so we grudgingly pay that penalty to make sure we can exercise this real-world feature.

Notice we use the self() for the notification pid, just as we did within IEx. We'll be able to use it to check for the notification messages as the server goes through its paces.

Now that the setup is behind us, we can test the quiz as it goes through the various parts of its lifecycle, like this:

```
BoundaryTests/test/proctor_test.exs
refute Mastery.take_quiz(quiz.title, email)
```

We initially make sure the quiz is not available. Remember, Mastery.take_quiz will return a nil if it's not yet scheduled.

Once we verify that this condition is satisfied, we can use the :started notification we just added, like this:

```
BoundaryTests/test/proctor_test.exs
assert_receive {:started, :timed_addition}
assert Mastery.take_quiz(quiz.title, email)
```

We make sure that the test receives the :started notification for the :timed_addition quiz, and then we take the quiz again, ensuring that we get a value back.

Next, we'll make sure the test terminates as we expect. Once again, we can use the notification again, like this:

```
BoundaryTests/test/proctor_test.exs
    assert_receive {:stopped, :timed_addition}
    assert [ ] == QuizSession.active_sessions_for(quiz.title)
  end
end
```

We get the notifications and then assert that the active sessions are in fact empty, and we're done. We need only run the test to make sure we're clean and green:

```
➜ mix test test/proctor_test.exs
.

Finished in 0.1 seconds
1 test, 0 failures
```

The test runs, and it runs quickly! We can use our notify_pid feature to keep our tests running quickly without requiring sleeps and intricate timing. There's no doubt that adding timing elements to our GenServer has a significant impact in the complexity of our tests. Mercifully, we're *only testing one aspect* of the quiz, the time-based lifecycle we introduce within our worker code. If we had done a poor job of separating the boundary and core of our code, we'd have to deal with all of those elements at once within our tests so our job would have been much more difficult.

We've finished up our test and all of the code for the book! We're ready to conclude this chapter.

Test Your Boundary

This chapter has gone quickly. We built an integration test to work through the base mastery.exs API. We built only a single test, but it covered an end-to-end scenario with persistence enabled and a quiz. We even built in enough wrong and right answers to show that our mastery feature was working.

Next, we dove into specific persistence tests. We wrote tests to call our basic persistence function two different ways. Then we simulated an exception and followed that up with a brief test of our reporting function.

Along the way we experienced the impacts of the layering strategy we've used throughout this book. In particular, for each API we were able to isolate the concerns of our test to one sliver of complexity. After all, that's the purpose of this whole book.

Good layering does not remove complexity. Instead, layering selectively limits the issues programmers have to deal with at any given time.

So do fun things with big, loud worker-bees. Build your projects in layers that expose the right complexity at the right time within your OTP projects. It's time to close the book and open up your editor to build something. We can't wait to see what you'll create!

Thanks for joining us.

—James and Bruce

Bibliography

[Heb19]   Fred Hebert. *Property-Based Testing with PropEr, Erlang, and Elixir*. The Pragmatic Bookshelf, Raleigh, NC, 2019.

[Mar08]   Robert C. Martin. *Clean Code: A Handbook of Agile Software Craftsmanship*. Prentice Hall, Englewood Cliffs, NJ, 2008.

[Tat18]   Ben Marx, José Valim, Bruce Tate. *Adopting Elixir*. The Pragmatic Bookshelf, Raleigh, NC, 2018.

[Tho18]   Dave Thomas. *Programming Elixir 1.6*. The Pragmatic Bookshelf, Raleigh, NC, 2018.

[TV19]   Chris McCord, Bruce Tate and José Valim. *Programming Phoenix 1.4*. The Pragmatic Bookshelf, Raleigh, NC, 2019.

[WM19]   Darin Wilson and Eric Meadows-Jönsson. *Programming Ecto*. The Pragmatic Bookshelf, Raleigh, NC, 2019.

Index

Thank you!

How did you enjoy this book? Please let us know. Take a moment and email us at support@pragprog.com with your feedback. Tell us your story and you could win free ebooks. Please use the subject line "Book Feedback."

Ready for your next great Pragmatic Bookshelf book? Come on over to https://pragprog.com and use the coupon code BUYANOTHER2020 to save 30% on your next ebook.

Void where prohibited, restricted, or otherwise unwelcome. Do not use ebooks near water. If rash persists, see a doctor. Doesn't apply to *The Pragmatic Programmer* ebook because it's older than the Pragmatic Bookshelf itself. Side effects may include increased knowledge and skill, increased marketability, and deep satisfaction. Increase dosage regularly.

And thank you for your continued support,

Andy Hunt, Publisher

Programming Elm

Elm brings the safety and stability of functional pro-
graming to front-end development, making it one of
the most popular new languages. Elm's functional nature and static typing means that runtime errors are
nearly impossible, and it compiles to JavaScript for
easy web deployment. This book helps you take advantage of this new language in your web site development.
Learn how the Elm Architecture will help you create
fast applications. Discover how to integrate Elm with
JavaScript so you can update legacy applications. See
how Elm tooling makes deployment quicker and easier.

Jeremy Fairbank
(308 pages) ISBN: 9781680502855. $40.95
https://pragprog.com/book/jfelm

Technical Blogging, Second Edition

Successful technical blogging is not easy but it's also
not magic. Use these techniques to attract and keep
an audience of loyal, regular readers. Leverage this
popularity to reach your goals and amplify your influence in your field. Get more users for your startup or
open source project, or simply find an outlet to share
your expertise. This book is your blueprint, with step-
by-step instructions that leave no stone unturned.
Plan, create, maintain, and promote a successful blog
that will have remarkable effects on your career or
business.

Antonio Cangiano
(336 pages) ISBN: 9781680506471. $47.95
https://pragprog.com/book/actb2

Build Chatbot Interactions

The next step in the evolution of user interfaces is here. Chatbots let your users interact with your service in their own natural language. Use free and open source tools along with Ruby to build creative, useful, and unexpected interactions for users. Take advantage of the Lita framework's step-by-step implementation strategy to simplify bot development and testing. From novices to experts, chatbots are an area in which everyone can participate. Exercise your creativity by creating chatbot skills for communicating, information, and fun.

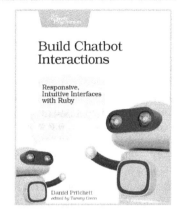

Daniel Pritchett
(206 pages) ISBN: 9781680506327. $35.95
https://pragprog.com/book/dpchat

Test-Driven React

You work in a loop: write code, get feedback, iterate. The faster you get feedback, the faster you can learn and become a more effective developer. Test-Driven React helps you refine your React workflow to give you the feedback you need as quickly as possible. Write strong tests and run them continuously as you work, split complex code up into manageable pieces, and stay focused on what's important by automating away mundane, trivial tasks. Adopt these techniques and you'll be able to avoid productivity traps and start building React components at a stunning pace!

Trevor Burnham
(190 pages) ISBN: 9781680506464. $45.95
https://pragprog.com/book/tbreact

Small, Sharp Software Tools

The command-line interface is making a comeback.
That's because developers know that all the best features of your operating system are hidden behind a
user interface designed to help average people use the
computer. But you're not the average user, and the
CLI is the most efficient way to get work done fast.
Turn tedious chores into quick tasks: read and write
files, manage complex directory hierarchies, perform
network diagnostics, download files, work with APIs,
and combine individual programs to create your own
workflows. Put down that mouse, open the CLI, and
take control of your software development environment.

Brian P. Hogan
(326 pages) ISBN: 9781680502961. $38.95
https://pragprog.com/book/bhcldev

Programming Ecto

Languages may come and go, but the relational
database endures. Learn how to use Ecto, the premier
database library for Elixir, to connect your Elixir and
Phoenix apps to databases. Get a firm handle on Ecto
fundamentals with a module-by-module tour of the
critical parts of Ecto. Then move on to more advanced
topics and advice on best practices with a series of
recipes that provide clear, step-by-step instructions
on scenarios commonly encountered by app developers.
Co-authored by the creator of Ecto, this title provides
all the essentials you need to use Ecto effectively.

Darin Wilson and Eric Meadows-Jönsson
(242 pages) ISBN: 9781680502824. $45.95
https://pragprog.com/book/wmecto

Web Development with ReasonML

ReasonML is a new, type-safe, functional language that compiles to efficient, readable JavaScript. ReasonML interoperates with existing JavaScript libraries and works especially well with React, one of the most popular front-end frameworks. Learn how to take advantage of the power of a functional language while keeping the flexibility of the whole JavaScript ecosystem. Move beyond theory and get things done faster and more reliably with ReasonML today.

J. David Eisenberg
(208 pages) ISBN: 9781680506334. $45.95
https://pragprog.com/book/reasonml

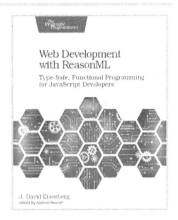

Programming WebAssembly with Rust

WebAssembly fulfills the long-awaited promise of web technologies: fast code, type-safe at compile time, execution in the browser, on embedded devices, or anywhere else. Rust delivers the power of C in a language that strictly enforces type safety. Combine both languages and you can write for the web like never before! Learn how to integrate with JavaScript, run code on platforms other than the browser, and take a step into IoT. Discover the easy way to build cross-platform applications without sacrificing power, and change the way you write code for the web.

Kevin Hoffman
(238 pages) ISBN: 9781680506365. $45.95
https://pragprog.com/book/khrust

The Ray Tracer Challenge

Brace yourself for a fun challenge: build a photorealistic 3D renderer from scratch! It's easier than you think. In just a couple of weeks, build a ray tracer that renders beautiful scenes with shadows, reflections, brilliant refraction effects, and subjects composed of various graphics primitives: spheres, cubes, cylinders, triangles, and more. With each chapter, implement another piece of the puzzle and move the renderer that much further forward. Do all of this in whichever language and environment you prefer, and do it entirely test-first, so you know it's correct. Recharge yourself with this project's immense potential for personal exploration, experimentation, and discovery.

Jamis Buck
(290 pages) ISBN: 9781680502718. $45.95
https://pragprog.com/book/jbtracer

Docker for Rails Developers

Docker does for DevOps what Rails did for web development—it gives you a new set of superpowers. Gone are "works on my machine" woes and lengthy setup tasks, replaced instead by a simple, consistent, Docker-based development environment that will have your team up and running in seconds. Gain hands-on, real-world experience with a tool that's rapidly becoming fundamental to software development. Go from zero all the way to production as Docker transforms the massive leap of deploying your app in the cloud into a baby step.

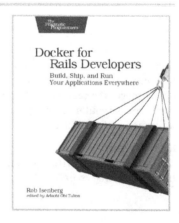

Rob Isenberg
(238 pages) ISBN: 9781680502732. $35.95
https://pragprog.com/book/ridocker

Practical Security

Most security professionals don't have the words "security" or "hacker" in their job title. Instead, as a developer or admin you often have to fit in security alongside your official responsibilities — building and maintaining computer systems. Implement the basics of good security now, and you'll have a solid foundation if you bring in a dedicated security staff later. Identify the weaknesses in your system, and defend against the attacks most likely to compromise your organization, without needing to become a trained security professional.

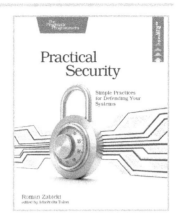

Roman Zabicki
(132 pages) ISBN: 9781680506341. $26.95
https://pragprog.com/book/rzsecur

Programming Crystal

Crystal is for Ruby programmers who want more performance or for developers who enjoy working in a high-level scripting environment. Crystal combines native execution speed and concurrency with Ruby-like syntax, so you will feel right at home. This book, the first available on Crystal, shows you how to write applications that have the beauty and elegance of a modern language, combined with the power of types and modern concurrency tooling. Now you can write beautiful code that runs faster, scales better, and is a breeze to deploy.

Ivo Balbaert and Simon St. Laurent
(244 pages) ISBN: 9781680502862. $35.95
https://pragprog.com/book/crystal

Genetic Algorithms and Machine Learning for Programmers

Self-driving cars, natural language recognition, and online recommendation engines are all possible thanks to Machine Learning. Now you can create your own genetic algorithms, nature-inspired swarms, Monte Carlo simulations, cellular automata, and clusters. Learn how to test your ML code and dive into even more advanced topics. If you are a beginner-to-intermediate programmer keen to understand machine learning, this book is for you.

Frances Buontempo
(234 pages) ISBN: 9781680506204. $45.95
https://pragprog.com/book/fbmach

Property-Based Testing with PropEr, Erlang, and Elixir

Property-based testing helps you create better, more solid tests with little code. By using the PropEr framework in both Erlang and Elixir, this book teaches you how to automatically generate test cases, test stateful programs, and change how you design your software for more principled and reliable approaches. You will be able to better explore the problem space, validate the assumptions you make when coming up with program behavior, and expose unexpected weaknesses in your design. PropEr will even show you how to reproduce the bugs it found. With this book, you will be writing efficient property-based tests in no time.

Fred Hebert
(374 pages) ISBN: 9781680506211. $45.95
https://pragprog.com/book/fhproper

Forge Your Future with Open Source

Free and open source is the foundation of software development, and it's built by people just like you. Discover the fundamental tenets that drive the movement. Take control of your career by selecting the right project to meet your professional goals. Master the language and avoid the pitfalls that typically ensnare new contributors. Join a community of like-minded people and change the world. Programmers, writers, designers, and everyone interested in software will make their mark through free and open source software contributions.

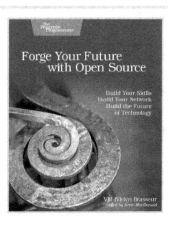

VM (Vicky) Brasseur
(222 pages) ISBN: 9781680503012. $33.95
https://pragprog.com/book/vbopens

Code with the Wisdom of the Crowd

Build systems faster and more effectively with Mob Programming. Mob Programming is an approach to developing software that radically reduces defects and key-person dependencies by having a group of people work together at a single machine. See how to avoid the most common pitfalls that teams make when first starting out. Discover what it takes to create and support a successful mob. Take collaborative programming to the next level!

Mark Pearl
(122 pages) ISBN: 9781680506150. $26.95
https://pragprog.com/book/mpmob

The Pragmatic Bookshelf

The Pragmatic Bookshelf features books written by developers for developers. The titles continue the well-known Pragmatic Programmer style and continue to garner awards and rave reviews. As development gets more and more difficult, the Pragmatic Programmers will be there with more titles and products to help you stay on top of your game.

Visit Us Online

This Book's Home Page
https://pragprog.com/book/jgotp
Source code from this book, errata, and other resources. Come give us feedback, too!

Keep Up to Date
https://pragprog.com
Join our announcement mailing list (low volume) or follow us on twitter @pragprog for new titles, sales, coupons, hot tips, and more.

New and Noteworthy
https://pragprog.com/news
Check out the latest pragmatic developments, new titles and other offerings.

Save on the eBook

Save on the eBook versions of this title. Owning the paper version of this book entitles you to purchase the electronic versions at a terrific discount.

PDFs are great for carrying around on your laptop—they are hyperlinked, have color, and are fully searchable. Most titles are also available for the iPhone and iPod touch, Amazon Kindle, and other popular e-book readers.

Buy now at *https://pragprog.com/coupon*

Contact Us

Online Orders:	*https://pragprog.com/catalog*
Customer Service:	*support@pragprog.com*
International Rights:	*translations@pragprog.com*
Academic Use:	*academic@pragprog.com*
Write for Us:	*http://write-for-us.pragprog.com*
Or Call:	+1 800-699-7764

CPSIA information can be obtained
at www.ICGtesting.com
Printed in the USA
BVHW082224301119
565279BV00007B/128/P